Faith for Personal Crises by Carl Michalson
Christianity and the Existentialists, edited by Carl Michalson

THE HINGE OF HISTORY

THE HINGE

OF

HISTORY

An Existential Approach
to the Christian Faith

BY

CARL MICHALSON

CHARLES SCRIBNER'S SONS

NEW YORK

ACKNOWLEDGMENTS

Some of the material in this book has appeared in the following magazines:
Religion in Life (under the titles "Existential Freedom and Christian Faith"
and "The Hinge of History"); *The Journal of Religion* (under the title
"Between Nature and God"); *Motive* (under the title "Communicating the
Gospel"); *Union Seminary Quarterly Review* (under the title "What Existen-
tialism Is About"); *Theology of Today* (under the titles "Communicating the
Gospel" and "Existentialism Is a Mysticism"). Copyright 1952, 1956, 1955,
1957, 1958 by Carl Michalson.

Chapters 5 and 6 have been adapted from Chapter 9 of *Faith and Ethics*,
edited by Paul Ramsey, with the permission of Harper & Brothers.

The quotation on page 19 from *Flaubert and Madame Bovary* by Francis
Steegmuller is used by permission of Alfred A. Knopf, Inc.

TO MY MOTHER

Mulier Timens Dominum

PREFACE

THE HINGE OF HISTORY is an introduction to theology in the sense that it projects a method of thinking about the Christian faith. In theology today the method has come to be known as existential interpretation. It is based upon what it means to say that Christianity is historical. Theology developed along the lines of this method would be theology conceived as history.

Traditionally, theology has adopted its methods of reflection from philosophy. More recently theologians have employed methods suggested by the natural sciences, as in American process theology. This book, however, proposes historical method as an instrument of theological understanding. The result is a theology of correlation. Unlike Paul Tillich's correlation, historiography and not ontology is made the foundation for the relation between divine and human concerns. Ontology and the natural process are not eliminated by history. History is simply placed at the center and given priority, as is not the case in such prevailing theologies as Tillich's and the naturalism of process theology. Furthermore, because the historiography involved is informed by the historical character of the Christian faith, the method should meet the usual objections which Barthians level against all forms of correlation.

The introductory chapter attempts to overcome some of the current ambiguity in the use of the term, "history," by specifying

9

four distinct kinds of history. The volume then divides into two parts. Part One developes *existential history* as the exposition of the meaninglessness in *world history*. Part Two develops *eschatological history* as the appearance of ultimate meaning through *Biblical history*. The concluding chapter defines the mission of the church which is implied in its eschatological faith.

The substance of this volume has been developed over the last seven years. Many of the suggestions in the volume have already been tried out in another form. Some of the content of Chapter 2 appeared in the *Journal of Religion*, October, 1955. Chapters 3 and 7 had their beginning in articles appearing in *Religion in Life* in Autumn, 1952, and Spring, 1956. Chapters 5 and 6 are written against the background of my contribution to *Faith and Ethics*, edited by Paul Ramsey and published by Harper and Brothers in 1957.

Chapters 4 and 9 are substantially the same as the articles by me in *Theology Today*, October, 1955, and October, 1957. Some of Chapter 9 also appeared in *Motive* in March, 1957. Chapter 10 includes material published by the *International Review of Missions*, April, 1956. My article in the *Union Seminary Quarterly Review* of January, 1958, has informed Chapters 3 and 5. Chapter 1 has appeared in Japanese in a volume in honor of the theologian, Ken Ishiwara, and Chapter 8 has come out in Japanese in Tokyo Union Theological Seminary's *Journal of Theology*, Number XV, 1959. I am greatly indebted to the editors of these periodicals and volumes for their permission to draw upon materials they have introduced.

Among those who have helped me in so many ways to complete this work I must thank Miss Pat Patterson of Aoyama Gakuin University in Tokyo for reading the entire manuscript and making valuable suggestions for improvement in expression; Miss Umeki Ushioda of Aoyama who typed the manuscript; Professor Yoshio Noro of the Aoyama and Tokyo Union Theological faculties for endless assistance during the final period of its composition; and to Mrs. Pat Winters for helping with the proofs and the index.

In this book I have tried to say *what it means that Christianity is historical*. At the very least, I believe it means that while one is reading a book about the faith he should not be distracted by indifferent matters which require him to suspend his existence. He should feel his life affected. In writing these pages, therefore, I have tried to be sensitive to Marcel Proust's warning that "a book in which there are theories is like an article from which the price mark has not been removed."

Carl Michalson

Drew Forest
Madison, N. J.

CONTENTS

THE HINGE OF HISTORY

INTRODUCTION

"Beneath us the earth is trembling. Where can we place our fulcrum, even admitting that we possess the lever? The thing we all lack is not style, nor that dexterity of finger and bow known as talent. We have a large orchestra, a rich palette, a variety of resources. We know many more tricks and dodges, probably, than were ever known before. No; what we lack is the intrinsic principle, the soul of the thing, the very idea of the subject. We take notes, we make journeys: emptiness! Emptiness! We become scholars, archaeologists, historians, doctors, cobblers, connoisseurs. What good is all that? Where is the heart, the verve, the sap? Where to start out from? Where to go to?"

—GUSTAVE FLAUBERT, *Letters*

CHAPTER

1

DIMENSIONS OF HISTORY

FIFTY years ago Ernst Troeltsch made a prediction which is just beginning to come true. He prophesied that if historical method were ever applied to the theological disciplines, it would become as a yeast, transforming and ultimately bursting the whole lump of customary theological procedure.[1] It is now virtually a commonplace to say that the Hebrew-Christian faith is basically historical. "In Israel, all religion is history" (Martin Buber) and "All theology is history." (Théo Preiss) Christianity has to do with "religious doctrines which are at the same time historical events." (Herbert Butterfield) One can now say such things without the slightest sense of explosion in his theological ovens. They are interpreted as a reminder to the church that Christianity roots in history.

This is not the outcome Troeltsch had in mind, however. The formulation of the Christian faith has not yet been radically enough affected. Theology has not yet been deeply enough seized by the unique historiography implicit in the Christian faith. No sooner had the holy event of God in Christ occurred than it was wedged apart by two ways of looking at it. The meaning of the event did

[1] "Über historische und dogmatische Methode in der Theologie," *Gesammelte Schriften*, Vol. II, cited by Friedrich Gogarten, p. 341, "Theologie und Geschichte," *Zeitschrift für Theologie und Kirche*, Jahr. 50, Heft 3, 1953.

not originally lend itself to expression in historical terms. History in the Graeco-Roman world was a realm of relativities where everything was perishing. Therefore, the Christian theologians were tempted to frame the significance of the revelational event in terms of what their culture regarded as ultimate, the categories of a suprahistorical metaphysics. At the same time, the chroniclers of the Christian movement were forced by professional necessity to treat the faith as historical. They had no alternative but to adopt the historiographical methods extant in Graeco-Roman culture. But classical historiography pretended to no influence upon the world. "World" was a concept geographically defined, and its unities were achieved by soldiers, not by historians.

The holy event of God's revelation in Christ, however, occurred with power to transform the world. Theologians have unwittingly vitiated the force of that power by applying to the expression of its truth methods which are not sufficiently informed by the truth itself. On one side, theologians have been willing to articulate the faith in terms of a non-historical metaphysics, abstracting the saving event from its very occurrence. On the other side, theologians have been willing to banalize the expression of the faith by casting the truth of its events in the form of a history which only records results. The true wholeness of the Christian event is thus broken in two. On one side are metaphysical claims which transcend events; on the other side are historical records which trace events.

The very split is permanized in some of the cardinal dogmas of the church. Christ becomes two natures, one for the theologian as historian, the other for the theologian as metaphysician. The element in the eucharist becomes a parallelism of substance and accident. The metaphysician presides over the substance. The accident is a symbol of the chance facts of history. Both methods commit what Cleanth Brooks has called "the paraphrastic heresy." They discuss the saving event in a medium in which the event does not occur. Dismembering the event, they drain its vital power to repeat itself. Locating its meaning beyond history or recording its factuality in history's past, they muffle its influence upon the ongoing history of the world, leaving to states and armies the influence upon history rightly belonging to the church through preaching.

Is the Christian truth a supra-historical essence in an historical shell? Is the holy event of God in Christ, remembered in the eucharist, a nature miracle? Is it an event in our pedestrian history which can only be accounted for in terms of super-natural forces beyond and separable from the event in which it occurs? So regarded, adherence to the doctrines expressing these claims requires enforcement by the external authority of the church. The parallelisms in the doctrines vitiate the integral meanings of the faith, meanings which should need no "official" paraphrase. May it not rather be true that revelation happens where nothing but history happens, so that theology must look for nothing and believe in nothing which is not history?[2] That, indeed, would be theology √ historically conceived. It would not be theology *about* something historical, worked out in a non-historical medium. It would be theology *as* history, theology as a moment of history, albeit an abstract moment, which would itself give rise to history.

This, I believe, is what Troeltsch had in mind when he predicted that a proper historiography would transform the theological disciplines.[3] The idea was not invented by Troeltsch. The Protestant reformers had already sponsored it by the way they broke with the substantialistic metaphysics of medieval theology, elevating the more historical motifs of the Bible to theological prominence and abandoning the concept of faith as intellectual adherence to propositional beliefs. Schleiermacher was the first Protestant theologian, however, to attempt to formulate systematic theology on the basis of the new Protestant direction.[4] Inasmuch as the nineteenth-century historiography was deficient in the Christian sense of history, Schleiermacher's effort to delineate theology from religious

[2] Gogarten's insistence, "Theologie und Geschichte," *ibid.*, p. 391.
[3] Cf. his "Historismus und seine Probleme" in *Gesammelte Schriften*, Vol. III, Tübingen, 1922.
[4] Wilhelm Herrmann, *Systematic Theology*, Macmillan, 1927, p. 69.

experience resembled anthropology more than theology. Ironically, the initial blast of theology during the First World War days removed Schleiermacher from his position of influence in theology while at the same time perpetuating his authentic Protestant concern. Contemporary theology, with the benefit of a Biblically enlightened historiography, is now attempting what Schleiermacher tried without that method. It is endeavoring to express the Christian faith in the terms in which the faith occurs, which is history.

The promise of the Protestant Reformation would approach fulfillment theologically if theology were to enter into an expression of the Christian faith historically conceived, where the concept of history involved is allowed to be illuminated by the historiography implicit in the Christian faith itself. In this volume I do not pretend to assume the task of doing theology as history, but only to make suggestions as to how it may be possible to do so. By way of introduction I shall attempt in this chapter to outline what appears to me to be the historical structure implicit in the holy event with which Christianity is bound up. In the subsequent chapters I shall explore some elements in the concept of history which are most crucial for the realization of the Christian faith.

The structure of history takes on the aspect of a spectrum of meanings, dimensions of history inseparable in act, separable in abstraction, but separable in abstraction in such a way as to do no violence to their inseparability in act. Four dimensions within the structure of history will be delineated in order not so much of their ascending importance as of their ascending uniqueness for a Christian historiography.

I. THE EXISTENTIAL IN WORLD HISTORY

The first element in the spectrum is *world history*. This is what every historian knows about, having to do with the characteristics that all hold in common. It is also what inescapably makes every man his own historian. As Hegel once said, "Every man must learn in the short span of his own life the whole long journey of mankind."

World history is something which happens and is past. Nothing more elementary can be said of history than that. Yet this characteristic, nowhere contested, introduces notable refinements when applied to the formulation of Christian doctrine. Historical truth by this criterion has a beginning and an end. While it is in one sense transitory, it is in another sense irrevocable. It is not irrevocable as mathematical truths are irrevocable in their timelessness. Mathematical truths do not happen; they simply are. It is irrevocable in the timely sense, as Cleopatra's nose is irrevocable. If it had been longer, it would have changed the history of the world.

Again, history which happens and is past always has to do with the unique. Each event must be treated as individual, not unrelated to other events, but related in terms of its own integrity. It must not, therefore, be judged as the inquisitor in *Don Quixote* judged libraries; tiring of taking the books down one by one, he issued his judgments en masoo.

When history happens and becomes past, the conditions for the objective judgment of events are at their best. The original Greek meaning of the word "history" has just this connotation. "History" meant "research," and "research" seems enhanced by an objective distance. The passage of time supplies that distance. Something must have happened before it can be investigated. An historical science, in this sense, ought to be able to provide more objectivity than even the natural sciences, where the object is always a vital and growing thing. When something happens and is past, it is so objective it is dead. It cannot speak in the same way living objects speak when probed by experimental methods. It remains all that it can ever be. By that fact, history should be the strictest of the sciences.

There is one important barrier to carrying off that claim. While history by becoming past sets up the conditions for knowledge of an *object*, it militates against the conditions for *knowledge* of the object. History is not only a kind of event; it is a way of grasping events. History is not only an objective occurrence; it is the knowledge of occurrences. Hence, limiting the definition of history to an occurrence which happens and is past makes history as knowledge impossible. That history happens and becomes past can be recorded by scientific chronicles in terms of factualities, but historical knowledge is not thereby achieved. What has happened includes not simply the question, *"Did* it happen?" but the questions *"Why* did it happen?" and *"What* does it mean?"

That is to say, what happens and is past has an inner as well as an outer aspect, a deep as well as a superficial, a vertebral as well as an epidermal. The structure of history cannot be comprehended, then, from some position outside the events themselves. That effort would parallel the spectacle of the gnat theorizing about the interior structure of an elephant from a position somewhere upon its hide, an analogy popular with the British historian Macaulay.

The moment one asks the question of the meaning of an event he plunges into its heart and becomes a part of it himself. It ceases being a simple account of what has happened. It becomes, as H. Richard Niebuhr says, "the story of our life." The historian ceases being what Montaigne calls the simple sort who "have nothing of their own to mix with it." When the history teacher in *The Brothers Karamazov* warns his student not to talk about an historical event without first understanding what he means by it, he is inviting the student to turn history into a form of autobiography. It is not at all mysterious that Lenin should have learned more about France from the novels of Balzac than from all the history books. History for Lenin was not something that had come to pass, to be recorded in his brain. It was something he must bring to pass through the total impact of his life. This is history in its primary sense. Not that it has nothing to do with history in its popular, vulgar, "happened-and-is-past" sense. It is simply that in the understanding of the primary and inner depth of history, the outer side of the event loses its hegemony. The outer side is not thereby done away. It follows in the orbit of the inner as a burnt-out rocket follows in the orbit of the satellite it launched. But no one is in doubt about which side of the event sends off the signal.

Nor should it be thought that inner and outer are simply two ways of looking at some single event, some event which remains a third thing hidden in the background. Inner and outer are two distinct events. The difference between the events arises within completely different forms of spiritual activity. The question about the outer reality of an event and the question about the inner reality have really nothing in common. The very mode of apprehension of an event decides what kind of event it shall be. The attitude of the spectator makes the outer event possible (*Historie*); the attitude of the participant makes the inner event possible (*Geschichte*). One cannot move back and forth between the two attitudes without a radical sense of break in the nature of the event itself. The account of Peter walking on the water supports this thesis dramatically. Peter could not move from the attitude of trust in his Lord to the attitude of conjecture about the buoyancy of bodies without sinking into a radically different medium of existence.

What saves history as inner event from being reduced to sheer subjectivism? History as inner event is to be distinguished from both subjectivism and objectivism in history. It is not an event created by a subject, a knower. Nor is it an event defined by an object without reference to a subject. The former would be too inventive to correspond to the realities of history. The latter would be too detached to admit of history as knowledge. History refers to events in which subject and object exist in a mode of togetherness.

Every historical datum is there *for* someone. Every historical consciousness is a "consciousness of" something, intending a reality other than itself. The properly historical event is neither the subject nor the object, but the point at which subject and object come together "intentionally." The locus of history is where the purpose of the object coincides with the consciousness of the subject. That mode of togetherness is what is meant by historical "understanding," "meaning," "interpretation." The historian in this view is not one who asks what has happened in history, nor how he should feel about what has happened. He asks for the meaning. That is the properly historical event.

The concept of "meaning," however, must not be drawn back into the subjectivistic orbit, as if it connotes "meaning *to* me." The historian does not state what is the meaning *to* him, but what is the meaning *for* him. The meaning has an integrity of its own, *extra nos*, which corresponds to our quest for meaning but is not constituted by our quest for meaning. Nor ought one suspect that the word "meaning" is tinctured by intellectualism, which would smack of a new kind of objectivism. For meanings which the historian delineates in the mode of togetherness between subject and object are not to be offered and appropriated as conceptual objects merely. That would tempt history into dogmatism. History as "meaning" has the task of setting up the conditions for meaningful existence in history. Meaning which is won in a mode of togetherness between subject and object can only be renewed in that same mode.[1]

Secular historians who refer to "written history as an act of faith" (Charles A. Beard) only appear to be saying the same thing as Christians. Actually, the relatedness of faith is not a relativism which vitiates the independent reality of the historical datum by the viewer's private standpoint. It is a relativism which deliberately lets the reality investigated speak for itself. History's category of inner participation like theology's category of faith has nothing to

[1] The hermeneutical method of Wilhelm Dilthey, Joachim Wach, and Rudolf Bultmann must be held together with the phenomenology of Edmund Husserl as revised away from natural science in the direction of historiography by Max Scheler, Martin Heidegger, and Maurice Merleau-Ponty.

do with private opinion. It is a method of letting reality deliver its meaning in a way it cannot under the less sensitive obstetrical methods of the objective grasp of outer history. Neither outer history nor inner history can be satisfied that Bancroft had the engravers remove the wart from Franklin's nose or that Jared Sparks edited the grammatical errors out of Washington's letters for publication. The weakness of outer history is not in its factual accuracy, but only in its pretension to arrive at the truth of history by factual means.

All history, therefore, insofar as it is inner history, is contemporary history. History in this sense is not an objective event which can be interpreted. The interpretation *is* the properly historical event. That "children should honor their parents" is true in this historical dimension only when some child is affirming it.[2] This seems clearly suggested in the biblical handling of the holy event of the cross. There is a cross in the sense in which John's gospel speaks of it: the executioner's weapon. This is history in its outer sense. But there is the cross in the sense in which Paul speaks of it when he uses the word *stauros*. That word does not mean the instrument of torture jointly sponsored by Rome and Judaism. It means "God was in Christ reconciling the world unto himself." That is the cross as gospel, as primary history. When John wishes to express that meaning he does so not with the use of the word "cross," but with the meaningful statement, "If I be lifted up I will draw all men unto me."

The historian can never get to the cross in its primary sense by way of the cross in its secondary sense. Time has removed the secondary history to an objective distance but has left no adequate handle by which to snatch it back into the present. The cross in its primary sense, however, can be recovered without the secondary history. This is the main significance of Christian reliance upon the apostolic tradition. The same historiographical structures

[2] Cf. Rudolf Bultmann, *Glauben und Verstehen*, Vol. I, Tübingen, 1933, p. 116, n. 2.

which made the cross primary for the apostles can make it contemporary for us. Their faith, which is the *meaning* of the cross,
can be (to use the word of R. G. Collingwood) re-enacted by us.
Henceforth there need be no discipleship second-hand. Their faith
becomes our access to the meaning of the cross for us. Their confession is the rock upon which Christ has built his church. What
R. G. Collingwood says on behalf of anyone's historiography is
ingredient in the Christian historiography (excepting, of course,
the evident traces of his mentalistic bias):

> The peculiarity which makes (an event) historical is
> not the fact of its happening in time, but the fact of its
> being known to us by our re-thinking the same thought
> which created the situation we are investigating, and thus
> coming to understand that situation.[3]

To say it as Melanchthon said it, "To know Christ is to know
his benefits." The Greek Orthodox theologian, John of Damascus,
ought not be blamed, of course, for announcing at the outset of
his theological *summa*, "I will say nothing of my own." The implicit historiography of the Christian faith had not quite caught
up with theological expression by the eighth century. Now, however, Christian historiography has caught up with even the secular
historians of our time. Formally speaking, nothing I have said thus
far concerning history would be unacceptable to the bulk of historians who deal in world history. A quick glance at methodological statement by contemporary historians, such as is given in Fritz
Stern's anthology, *Varieties of History*, would show an impressive
consensus on these perspectives. "History . . . is the self-consciousness of humanity—humanity's effort to understand itself through
the study of its past." (Turner) "History is humanity's knowledge
of itself, its certainty about itself." (Droysen) History ought to
"help us to understand ourselves and our fellows and the problems
and prospects of mankind." (Robinson) History is "the exposition
of these facts and opinions in their full emotional and intellectual

[3] *The Idea of History*, Oxford, 1946, p. 218.

value to a wide public by the difficult art of literature." (Trevelyan) "The history of civilization, if intelligently conceived, may be an instrument of civilization." (Beard)[4]

The historians who do refuse to go this far will probably do so out of failure to distinguish adequately between nature and history. Nature by definition is the world in so far as it is silent about the meaning of man. History is the world in so far as the question about the possibility of a meaningful life is opened up.[5] If that be the case, it would be a damaging judgment for one to say, as Collingwood does, that in the past historians have uniformly treated history as if it were nature.[6] By his own confession, for instance, the nineteenth-century French historian Taine observed his subject "as one might observe the metamorphosis of an insect."[7] Walter Rauschenbusch's evolutionary view of history surely had something to do with the fact that he came to the teaching of church history from the teaching of zoology. What if it were true, then, as Paul Tillich says it is, that the choice between nature and history is a decision "against or for Christianity?"[8] It would simply mean that it is possible for historians by a wrong historical method to scan the past and never stumble upon a Christian possibility. It could mean as well, however, that theologians, articulating the faith by categories which do not reflect the distinction between nature and history, could thwart the coming of faith. In that light, one can see how serious Rudolf Bultmann's charge is when he says of Oscar Cullmann's book *Christ and Time* that Cullmann makes no distinction between the historical process and the natural event.[9]

---

[4] *Op. cit.*, Meridian, 1956, pp. 297, 144, 261, 236, 314, respectively.
[5] Cf. p. 66, Ernst Fuchs, *Hermeneutik*, Bad Cannstatt, 1954.
[6] *The Idea of History*, p. 175.
[7] Quoted by Eric Voegelin, *Order and History*, Vol. I, Louisiana State University Press, 1956, p. 59.
[8] *The Protestant Era*, Chicago University Press, 1948, p. 17.
[9] Vide "Heilsgeschichte und Geschichte," *Theologische Literaturzeitung*, 1948, No. 11.

At this juncture let us test our comprehension of this specialized sense in which history is being used today. Is it right to be preoccupied with history to the exclusion of nature? Does not Christ become in some sense nature when he takes on flesh? Do not all things, including nature, cohere in him? Does not the whole creation, that is, history *and* nature, travail together until now? Or to put it as Jacques Maritain has done, does not the cherry between one's lips hold more mystery than the whole idealist metaphysic?

One who has followed this discussion will sense a possible equivocation with the word "nature." Nature does not mean simply the birds and the bees. It refers rather to anything that does not involve one's life in the question of meaning. In that sense, what is often called history can be but nature: it does not involve our lives in the question of meaning. Likewise, what is often classified exclusively as nature can be productive of history. The cherry between one's lips, for instance, can be nature or history, depending upon how one relates to it. For the wine merchant it will be one thing. For the poet it will be another, if he says, pinching out its juices between his teeth,

> I hold you here, pit and all, in my lips,
> Little cherry—but *if* I could understand
> What you are, pit and all, and all in all,
> I should know what God and man is.

The attitude converts a potential natural event into an actual historical event.

Theologians faithful to the classical doctrine of the incarnation make a mistake, therefore, to suggest that the category of inner history is a threat to the embodiment affirmed in Christian realities.[10] They feel that the historical Jesus, his resurrection, and his

---

[10] E.g., Hans Frei, "The Theology of H. Richard Niebuhr," in *Faith and Ethics*, edited by Paul Ramsey, Harpers, 1957; R. R. Niebuhr, *Resurrection and Historical Reason*, Scribners, 1958; Claude Welch, *The Reality of the Church*, Scribners, 1958, esp. pp. 38, 65, and 115. These volumes are refreshing and stunning evidence of the importance of historiography in contemporary theological method. Evidence is lacking in these works, however,

embodiment in the church surrender their substantive character to
the inner event so that the incarnational faith is jeopardized. It is
a confusion of great seriousness, however, to believe that the embodiment of God's word in history is there as an object alike of
outer and inner history. It can be an object for both, but not alike
for both. The embodied church, for instance, seen by inner history
is not the same church as the embodied church seen by outer history. Inner history simply brackets out the question of the empirical,
outer-historical existence of christological and ecclesiological realities. The question of outer history is not yet a properly historical
question. It is a nature question. Inner history asks the question of
meaning. Now, the answer to the question of meaning may well
be, and in these instances *is*, that embodiment is of the essence of
the reality. But the embodiment concluded from the question of
meaning is not the same as the embodiment adduced without that
question. Inner history does not reduce the nature of Christ or his
church to a subjective reality, leaving his embodiment to an outer
history which is forced to play an insignificant role. Inner history
asserts that the embodiment of Christ and the church simply cannot be grasped by the methods of outer history. Christians concede
that in their creeds when, notwithstanding his embodiment, they
say "I believe . . . in Jesus Christ," and, notwithstanding its empirical obtrusiveness, "I believe . . . (in) the . . . Church." The
embodied realities of the Christian faith are always the object of
faith, that is, of inwardly oriented understanding.

The task of the historian, then, involves him in raising the question of meaning, which is the properly historical question. The
ability to find meaning in history, however, is contingent upon
one's finding continuity between events. Being an historian is

---

that the authors understand how "neo-Kantian" subjectivism is corrected in
contemporary existentialism by Dilthey's hermeneutic and Husserl's phenomenology. The same oversight is evident in Europe in the work of Helmut
Thielicke and Hermann Diem, both of whom characterize their theology as
"the way between historicism and existentialism," as if existentialism's
method of subjectivity were a subjectivism.

closely tied up with being a man, for to be a man is to possess the interest and the capacity to make judgments which hold many moments together in meaningful sequence. "It snows. The sun shines. The snow melts." As an animal, man can simply luxuriate in each isolated moment of that succession. As a man, he must sooner or later cry out, "Aha! When the sun shines the snow melts." By that judgment he pulls three moments of life into a single meaning. This passion for connecting things partly explains historical research and such auxiliary arms of history as archaeology. Hitherto unknown links in human history simply must be supplied.

But what if the continuity in events is not obvious, is not extrinsic? And what if the historian, entering into events as the story of his life, feels the gaps in history as gaps in his very being? Under such circumstances the historian is most apt to become a philosopher of history. A philosopher of history fills the gaps in history with plausible explanations implied by history but not explicit there. Set two historical phenomena end to end: "Rome was great; Rome fell." These little pieces in the grand arch of time constitute world history. But the pieces do not fit. The question remains: How is the decline of Rome accounted for by its greatness? There is an evident chronological succession, but the significance which makes the succession history is not evident. What the historian does not see as historian he must put there as philosopher. The concern for meaningful life requires it.

The philosopher of history stuffs the holes in history with connections which allay the anxieties of the sensitive people for whom history is not simply the external spectacle but the stream of life in which they are themselves immersed. Arnold Toynbee has helped us understand Rome. When creative minorities are in power, responding to the challenge in the changing conditions of life, Rome remains great. When creative minorities become dominant minorities, they develop rigidity, fail to respond resiliently, and hence break upon developing conditions. However, this knowledge is not history; it is philosophy of history. But the aspect of history which is most apt to give rise to the philosophy of history is this compelling concern for meaning within world history which can be called existential history. Existential history is the dimension of history in which the cracks in the arch of world history are felt as some lack of completeness in one's own life, in one's own capacity to negotiate life with meaning.

> What is Rome?
> It decays.
> What is the world?
> It comes to nothing
> E'er thy towers carry domes,
> E'er thy shining stars ascend
> Out of miles of mosaic.
> —(RILKE, *Das Stundebuch*. First Book.)

John Donne's couplet describing seventeenth century life has the same historical force:

> Tis all in peeces,
> All cohaerence gone.

One may be seeing world history as a road segmented here and there by washouts or as a vessel riddled in its hull by holes. World history becomes existential history the moment one sees oneself as already embarked upon that broken course, already afloat upon that ship.

Existential history refers to what I would like to call the paratactic structure in history. "Paratactic" is a word which usually applies to sentences deficient in connectives. The sentences just seem placed alongside each other. There is no sign of syntax, of connectedness. They are, that is, paratactic. The novels of Virginia Woolf are filled with such structures. Take these two sentences from her story *To the Lighthouse*: One of her characters stands at a window, looking out. Virginia Woolf then writes, " 'The Mountains are so beautiful.' Her father was dying there."[11]

---

[11] Cited by Erich Auerbach, *Mimesis*, Anchor, 1957, p. 465. Used by permission of Princeton Univ. Press.

This is a paratactic structure. There is nothing in the first sentence which adequately accounts for the second. Christian literature is filled with paratactic. "God said, 'Let there be light.' And there was light." "Once I was blind. Now I see." "Jesus said, 'Follow me.' And he arose and followed him." "Some believed. Others doubted." "Jesus was crucified, dead, and buried. On the third day he rose from the dead." The paratactic structure is a literary way of acknowledging the gaps in history, gaps which may be described by what Henry Fielding has called in *The History of Tom Jones*, "blanks in the grand lottery of time."

The late Erich Auerbach has written suggestively of paratactic. In his influential work on "the representation of reality in Western literature," called *Mimesis*, he draws a contrast between classical and Biblical literature. In Homer's *Odyssey*

> the separate elements of a phenomenon are most clearly placed in relation to one another; a large number of conjunctions, adverbs, particles, and other syntactical tools, . . . a continuous rhythmic procession of phenomena passes by, and never is there a form left fragmentary or half-illuminated, never a lacuna, never a gap, never a glimpse of unplumbed depths.[12]

In the Bible, on the other hand, such as in the conversation between Abraham and Isaac, all is quite different.

The decisive points of the narrative alone are emphasized,

> what lies between is nonexistent; time and place are undefined and call for interpretation; thoughts and feeling remain unexpressed, are only suggested by the silence and the fragmentary speeches; the whole, permeated with the most unrelieved suspense and directed toward a single goal . . . remains mysterious and "fraught with background."[13]

Auerbach then suggests that this literary structure reflects reality so efficiently that by it you can tell when you are reading legend,

[12] *Ibid.*, p. 4.
[13] *Ibid.*, p. 9.

and when history. "Their structure is different."[14] History will have paratactic in it; thus the writing of history will reflect the paratactic.

> (Legend) runs far too smoothly. All cross-currents, all friction, all that is casual, secondary to the main events and themes, everything unresolved, truncated and uncertain, which confuses the clear progress of the action and the simple orientation of the actors, has disappeared. The historical event (on the other hand) runs much more variously, contradictorily, and confusedly; . . . To write history is so difficult that most historians are forced to make concessions to the technique of legend.[15]

Auerbach even goes so far as to suggest that the obviously legendary materials of the Old Testament have an historical base discernible from the very structure of the literature.

> Abraham, Jacob, or even Moses produces a more concrete, direct, and historical impression than the figures of the Homeric world . . . because the confused, contradictory multiplicity of events, the psychological and factual cross-purposes, which true history reveals, have not disappeared in the representation but still remain clearly perceptible.[16]

In the light of Auerbach's claim, it is a tribute to the historical sense of the early church that Tatian's smooth harmonizing of the four gospels, which he called the *Diatessaron*, was not accepted as canonical scriptures, but in its place the four separate gospels in all their unharmonized, paratactic starkness.

Two contemporary theologians have contributed insights which add greatly to the comprehension of history as paratactical. One is Reinhold Niebuhr's interpretation of irony in history. Irony exposes the paratactic which is the gap between our project and our achievements. Niebuhr has himself called this "the existentialist

---

[14] *Ibid.*, p. 16.
[15] *Ibid.*, pp. 16, 17.
[16] *Ibid.*, p. 17.

element" in history.[17] As he says, "Every sensitive individual has a relation to a structure which is never fulfilled" by him and he experiences this gap as irony.[18] Irony, then, becomes a paratactic symbol pointing beyond existential history to a fulfillment not accessible within history's ambiguities. Albert Camus' *The Fall* is a penetrating literary application of this symbol to contemporary history, dealing with the consternation of a man who watches his pedestrian righteousness cave in under the pressures of life.

Another valuable insight is Paul Tillich's interpretation of the demonic in history. The demonic is his way of accounting for the paratactic which is the gap between our efforts and our achievement, for the demonic is the existence in history of an active force of meaninglessness. It is a history-thwarting force. Where one event manifests a destructive force not explainable by the foregoing event or chain of events, there is a paratactic gap. Tillich fills this gap with his concept of the demonic, which "drives the personality beyond the limits of its allotted form to creations and destruction it cannot grasp as it own."[19] Camus also deals with this. *The Fall* is always the story of "the rebel" who out of a relatively innocent unwillingness to repent is overcome by the compulsion to commit murder.

What is at work in history, then, that some events cannot be explained by what precedes them? How does it happen that in one moment we are plunging through history with all the confidence of an ocean liner in the North Atlantic and in the next moment we are floundering in the sea with only a life boat under us? Who saw what happened? Who can piece together the fragments in the picture of our life? Without some witness who can fill that gap, we are doomed to what the poet Hölderlin called "the night of history," "the age of the absence of the Gods." "What man seeks

---

[17] *The Irony of American History*, Scribners, 1952, p. 164.

[18] *Ibid.*, p. 6. Cf. also Stanley Romaine Hopper, *The Crisis of Faith*, Abingdon, 1944.

[19] *The Interpretation of History*, Scribners, 1936, p. 81. Cf. also Edwin Lewis, *The Creator and the Adversary*, Abingdon, 1948.

in history is not life but reasons for living," as Camus has said.[20] Or, to say it as Gerhard Krüger does, "The problem of history in its extremest form is nihilism. . . . The deepest misery of history is man's anxiety over the possibility of a meaningful life."[21] One who places that kind of strain upon world events does not find it the least implausible for Paddy Chayevski in *The Goddess* to refer to the past as "the long parade of history that has brought us to this year of suicides and insanity."

The vision of history includes a paratactic vision, a seeing double, a condition in which meaning does not focus. But existential history is the refusal to live with equanimity in the presence of separated things. There is an implicit waiting for a witness who can introduce a unitary vision into a life disturbed by "a sense of the relation of separated things," (R. P. Blackmur) and by that vision make our on-going life seem justifiable.

> Things fall apart; the center cannot hold.
> . . . . Surely some revelation is at hand.
> (w. b. YEATS, "The Second Coming")

II. THE ESCHATOLOGICAL IN BIBLICAL HISTORY

Biblical history supplies what existential history finds lacking in world history. Biblical history is the witness to the occurrence of events in history which have the capacity to fill the paratactic gaps, to supply the revelation without which our life is all in pieces, all coherence gone. These are what might be called "the paradigmatic events." (Eric Voegelin) They are historical events which have a special role. They teach us something *about* history. More particularly, they are paradigmatic events in the sense that they are the events which more than any others provide the very form of our existence. Without such events, our life in history would be un-

[20] *The Rebel*, Vintage, 1956, p. 73.
[21] *Die Geschichte im Denken der Gegenwart*, Frankfurt, Wissenschaft und Gegenwart No. 16, 1947, pp. 11, 19. This significant essay also appears in *Grosse Geschichtsdenker*, edited by Rudolf Stadelmann, Tübingen, 1949.

justifiable. They are *mysterious events,* incapable of being accounted for by what precedes them. But they are mysterious in this
way precisely because they are *originating events,* having no pre-
history, and providing in themselves the meaning of all subsequent
events. Their truth is not determinable in relation to or by deri-
vation from other events. For they are themselves the events which
determine the meaning of all other events and from which all other
events derive their capacity to survive the paratactic threat of
meaninglessness.

These are the moments in history which, as Reinhold Niebuhr
says, "are more than mere historic moments [by which he means
world history]; for in them a whole course of history is fulfilled.
In them the seeming chaos of the past achieves its meaning; and
the partial and particular aspects of life are illumined to become
parts of a complete whole."[1] Or, as Martin Buber says, these are
the events which are "so enormous" that a people which meets
them "cannot ascribe them to its own plans and their realization,
but must perceive in them deeds performed by heavenly powers."[2]

> Something happens to us, the cause of which we cannot
> ascribe to our world; the event has taken place just now, we
> cannot understand it, we can only believe it (Exodus
> 14:31). It is a holy event.[3]

The comprehension of the paradigmatic structure of history
overshadows in Christian importance the popular distinction between outer and inner history, between nature categories and history categories within history. For inner and outer must be overlaid
by the much more fundamental distinction between history in
general and this special kind of holy history. There is what Luther
called the *historiae gentiles,* the profane history, and what he

[1] *Discerning the Signs of the Time,* Scribners, 1946, p. 96.
[2] "Saga and History," *The Writings of Martin Buber,* Will Herberg, editor,
Meridian, 1956, p. 152.
[3] "Holy Event," *ibid.,* p. 160.

called the *historiae sacrae*, the holy history.[4] The paradigm which supplies the authentic form of human existence is to be found in the holy history.

It is the awareness of history as paradigmatic which makes theologians impatient with every form of historicism. Historicism is not wrong because it pursues history, as Leopold von Ranke said we should, in order to determine nothing but objective facts. Someone must constantly be working at that enterprise. What happened and is past is nevertheless a kind of history. Historicism is wrong, however, in refusing to concede as a valid dimension of history events impervious to objective methods. For paradigmatic events are *intrinsically* inaccessible. The events of Biblical history are not the events one knows. They are the events *with the help of which one knows*. With them he knows, not knowing them, what he would not know without them. This is the reason they are called events of revelation. They occur with apocalyptic suddenness and with a luminousness which leaves the event itself unfathomed while illuminating the whole landscape of our life.

Biblical history, then, does not refer to events in general, but to special events. They are not unique in the sense of being isolated events. On the contrary, they are unique in supplying the hinges between events which would otherwise leave our lives in paratactic incompleteness. The Apostle Paul set out to make this clear to the Corinthians who mistook Christ's resurrection for an isolated event. Paul made it clear that this was rather the event by which their own resurrection was to be affirmed. The resurrection had been the very event by which Paul was enabled to see the crucifixion not as a paratactic defeat in history but as a holy victory.

Nor does Biblical history refer to factual events, but to trustworthy events. Biblical events are trustworthy not because they are factual, but because these are the events in which God makes accessible to us a justifiable life. The covenant on Sinai or the

[4] *Weimar Ausgabe* 14, 506f. Cf. Hans-Walter Krumwrede, *Glaube und Geschichte in der Theologie Luthers*, Göttingen, 1952.

resurrection of Jesus Christ are not binding on the worshipper because they happened in the irrevocable past. They are binding because they ground our faith. Biblical events are not really facts at all. In the extent to which they are facts they are still only world historical. We can unconditionally trust Biblical events because God is present to them in a way he is not to world history. Biblical events are not facts but mysteries which illuminate our paratactically porous facts. Biblical history is the witness which saves history from meaninglessness by reporting the clue to the mystery in history.

Biblical events are not historical, then, simply on the grounds on which world history is historical. Sinai is not historical simply because it happened and is past. Nor is it historical simply because it is now capable of being entered into inwardly so as to become contemporary. All that is world history. Biblically conceived, Sinai is historical because that event contributes to an entire people the very form of their existence. Similarly, the historicity of the Christian revelation *may* be asserted within the categories of world history, but to do so is an act of bad faith which undervalues the truth of the event which says Christ is the hinge of history, the paradigmatic event which supplies the very form of the Christian man's existence.

The task of the Biblical historian is, as St. Luke, historian among New Testament writers, says, "to compile" ($\dot{a}\nu a\tau \acute{a}\xi a\sigma\theta a\iota$). The historian restores ($\dot{a}\nu a$) to the historical tradition a connectedness of view ($\tau \acute{a}\xi\iota s$) by which one "may know the truth of the things of which you have been informed." (Luke 1:1-4) The author of John's gospel employs the same "anatactic" function. These things are written, he says, "that you may believe that Jesus is the Christ, the Son of God, and that believing you may have life in his name." (John 20:31)

What, then, shall the Christian witness to if he wishes to supply the links which save a man from falling through the gaps in history? He must be sure to witness to the mystery, which has the paradigmatic power. He must know what to report, as Mary knew after confronting the resurrected Lord. He must not return to his brethren with the exclamation, "The tomb was empty!" That would be at best the merest reiteration of a paratactic gap, at worst "the necromancy that sees in each precious object a mirror of the past."[5] He must announce instead that Jesus has ascended to his Father, that the Father of Jesus is God and that through him God has become their father. (John 20:17)

Even as I write these lines I feel somewhat tentative about what Christians are so widely standardizing in our time as "the Biblical view of history." A lingering paratactic threatens even this generalization. Nicolas Berdyaev put his finger on the feeling when he confessed that "Christian history finds itself in inner conflict with the Jewish spirit."[6] Rudolf Bultmann says the same less diplomatically: "For the Christian faith, the Old Testament is not revelation."[7] Is there not a paratactic gap between the Old and New Testaments which is not quite overcome by binding them in a single back? And does not that gap suggest a more specific conclusion about the Christian structure of history than merely the word "Biblical" can cover?

There is an evident continuity between the Old Testament and the New Testament. They represent two successive moments of a single plan. The Old Testament is progress toward that from which the New Testament is a continuation. Where this continuity is not trusted, docetism and gnosticism threaten the Christian faith with lack of seriousness about the paradigmatic character of history.[8] The God who acts in the Old Testament is the same God who acts in the New Testament. Each Testament knows history has a paradigmatic structure which holds that man must obey God's acts in history, making them the very form of his existence.

[5] Samuel Beckett, Proust, Evergreen, first published in 1931, p. 15.
[6] The Beginning and the End, Torchbook, 1957, p. 105.
[7] Glauben und Verstehen, Vol. I, p. 333.
[8] Karl Barth, Die kirchliche Dogmatik, IV, 1, Zürich, 1953, p. 183, and Oscar Cullmann, Christ and Time, Westminster, 1950, p. 56.

If that is what Paul Tillich means, he is right to say that in the Judeo-Christian tradition there is "identity of structure at all points."[9]

But Tillich is wrong to continue by saying there is "identity of content in most points." There is instead a disturbing discontinuity between the traditions which disallows to the Old Testament an independent status as the word of God. Does not the very name *"Old Testament"* presuppose a *"New"* which abrogates or recasts it?[10] Is not the Old Testament like an artist's sketch, no longer necessary now the completed statue is here?[11] Surely the New Testament ought not be understood simply as the consequence of an historical development. Even though a Christ is expected in the Old Testament, it is obvious in the New Testament that the Christ who came was not the Christ who was expected. Living in the Old Testament today should be analogous to a woman living in travail long after the baby has been born. It is true, of course, that Buber's criterion of a Jew is also the criterion of a Christian: "He who does not await the Messiah is not a true Jew." He is not a true Christian, either. But does not the Old Testament, taken by itself, canonize "waiting," hence infinitize it, hence make waiting an abstraction?[12] All that the Old Testament expects has been fulfilled in Christ. (Luke 4:21) Henceforth, a Christian's waiting goes on within the wake of Christ's appearing.

The Old Testament testifies to a plurality of paradigmatic events which taken together form a holy history, a *Heilsgeschichte*. The New Testament witnesses to the single event of God's action in Jesus Christ which happens with finality. Hereafter, to be a Christian is to have one's existence formed by that single event, a *Heilsgeschehen*. The finality of the event of Christ is not an attribute of its sheer occurrence in world history where every event

---

[9] "Is There a Judeo-Christian Tradition?" in *Judaism*, Vol. I, No. 2, April 1952.
[10] Henri de Lubac, *Histoire et Ésprit*, Paris, 1950, p. 281.
[11] Jean Daniélou, *Le mystère de l'Histoire*, Paris, 1953, p. 13.
[12] *Vide*, Karl Barth, *Die Kirchliche Dogmatik*, IV, 1, p. 101.

is final in its mere irrevocability. Its finality inheres in its completeness. World history may move ahead, but holy history is summed up here. There are no further paradigms to be expected by which a man may find the form of his existence.

Those who lived within the Old Testament faith in the days before our Lord lived by faith in his appearing and saw him from afar. (Hebrews 11:10, 13, 39) To continue to live within the Old Testament faith after his appearing is to see him no longer simply from a distance, but to see him from a disobedient distance. Stephen clarified this bluntly in an address in which he offered the appearing of Christ as the paradigm by which to read what previously passed in Israel for holy history. (Acts 7) Paul did the same for the Corinthians when he indicated that "only through Christ" can the veil be lifted not simply from history in general but even from the holy history of the old covenant. (2 Cor. 3:12-16) "What once had splendor has come to have no splendor at all, because of the splendor that surpasses it." (vs. 10)

John Calvin was as misleading as Tillich, then, to claim that "the covenant made with all the fathers" is the same as the new covenant in substance, differing only in execution.[13] He may even have been deficient in the sense of history. For paradigmatic acts require radical decision and obedience. The appearance of Christ is an event which supersedes all previous events and teleologically suspends all previous acts of obedience by an imperious claim to be the sole authentic form of all existence. Everything hinges on Christ. As the New Testament affirms, it is in Christ that all things now cohere. Luther shows a surer sense of history when he comments that one can believe in the Old Testament, but if one does not believe in Christ, it will not help him any.[14]

What I am contending for, then, is a teleological suspension of Biblical history by what might be called *eschatological history*. For the event of Christ is not just one more paradigm alongside other

13 *Institutes* II, 10, 2.
14 *Weimar Ausgabe* 23, 85.

Biblical events. It is the last paradigm, the ultimate paradigm by which all others are interpreted, the hinge by which all history hangs together. Christians receive the Old Testament from the hands of Jesus Christ. Henceforth, as the Old Testament scholar Gerhard von Rad has said, the way we will interpret it depends on what we think of Christ.[15]

Furthermore, Christians now receive the world itself from Jesus Christ. (Gal. 4:1-7) The Christian revelation is a "cosmic event," the event in which our whole existence finds its full summation. Hence, the very way we live through world history will depend on what we think of Christ. This particular holy event is not merely one more event in holy history. To call it "cosmic" is not simply to say it happens in the world. It happens in the world to end the world in its old form. It gives all history its end, its meaning. The new creation into which the Christian is ushered by this event is an historical reality, but it is history lived eschatologically. For here a whole new age has its beginning. (2 Cor. 5:17)

Of the four dimensions of history, those most frequently alluded to in contemporary theology are world history and Biblical history. A knowledge of these histories is, of course, indispensable to a theology which seeks to develop itself on the basis of histo-

[15] I am indebted to Bernard W. Anderson for this allusion. Cf. especially Wilhelm Vischer, "Das alte Testament und die Geschichte" in Zwischen den Zeiten, 10 Jahr., Heft 1, 1932; John Marsh, "Christ in the Old Testament" in Essays in Christology for Karl Barth, edited by T. H. L. Parker, Lutterworth Press, 1956. An impressive work has recently been completed in Japan by Zenda Watanabe on the interpretation of the Bible as the canon of the Church: The Doctrine of the Scriptures, Tokyo, Vol. I, 1949; Vol. II, 1954. The most provocative expression of this position is already taken in the Lukan materials of the New Testament according to Hans Conzelmann, Die Mitte der Zeit, Studien zur Theologie des Lukas, second edition, Tübingen, 1957. According to Luke, "the resurrection is the turning point. Since then, one can no longer appeal to ignorance. The Jew can no longer appeal to his non-Christian understanding of the scriptures! If he does, he has lost the scriptures—moreover the church appears as the legitimate heir of Israel. The scripture belongs to the church, for the church possesses the right interpretation." p. 140.

riography. World history tutors us in the distinction between outer and inner history and in the importance of making a place for history as a way of knowing which involves the knower himself in the pursuit of meaning. Biblical history tutors us in the role which particular events in history play in communicating the holy intention of God.

Strangely, however, the outer dimension of world history is unproductive of Christian faith. When world history is made synonymous with the whole of history, it can even militate against the arrival of faith. The inner dimension of world history is exceedingly important to Christianity, yet its importance is purely formal and not at all unique to Christianity. A Christian will participate in his history inwardly; but not everyone who participates in his history inwardly is a Christian. Biblical history provides a prehistory for the decisive Christian history as world history does not. Nevertheless, Biblical history is superseded by eschatological history. It is so radically superseded, one might almost say that eschatological history reduces Biblical history to the status of world history, or at least to the status of existential history. Biblical history has lost its substantial significance as saving history now that God is present in Christ as the hinge of history.

Existential history is no more unique to Christianity than world history. Yet it is prior to Christianity in much the same way Biblical history is in respect of the urgency of the quest for ultimate historical fulfillment. While existential history does not have the structural similarities to eschatological history which Biblical history has, it can be said to have within it the Christian intention.

Therefore, the aim of Part I of this volume will be to deal with existential history in such a way as to uncover the strain of urgency in world history. The aim of Part II will be to explore the elements in eschatological history which supply ultimacy and finality to the otherwise unconsummated process of Biblical history.

PART ONE

EXISTENTIAL HISTORY

"Midway the path of life that men pursue
I found me in a darkling wood astray,
For the direct way had been lost to view."

DANTE, *Inferno*, canto. 1, i-iii

"For the man of today the question of the true meaning
of life is no longer the most pressing problem. It is rather
the question whether there is a meaningful life at all, and
how it is possible to exist as a man, that is, in some meaningful way. . . . The problem of history is no longer merely
a question of thought but a question of one's being or
nothingness."

GERHARD KRÜGER, *Grundfragen der Philosophie*,
Frankfurt am Main, 1958, pp. 7, 77

MARTIN LUTHER once complained it was impossible to become a theologian except without the help of Aristotle, "that comedian who deluded the church with his Greek mask." In the church today, it has become increasingly difficult to be a theologian except with the help of existentialism. A great cry has gone up over this alliance, however. The Greek mask of the classical philosophies seems to hide an innocent face compared to what lies behind the mask of existentialism.

The classical philosophies at least saw an orderliness and symmetry in nature reminiscent of Psalmnody. Existentialism sees only chaos, as if before the time of the creation. The classical philosophies made man's highest act an act of reason, capable of knowledge. Existentialism sponsors passionate leaps, dignifying ignorance. Classical philosophies asserted a view of man which gave him status higher than the animal and even conceded immortality. Existentialism calls man "nothing" and says his life is a pilgrimage of unrelieved thirst. Classical philosophies believed in what the church could plausibly construe as God. Existentialism is atheistic. If Luther found Aristotle's pious insights hostile to the interests of the faith, how can existentialism acquire theological esteem today with its defiant and eccentric categories? The early church called Plato a Greek-speaking Moses. Could one, even in a frenzied moment, regard Sartre as a French-speaking Luther?

There are excellent grounds for seeing that the reformulation of the instruments of thought taking place in existentialism today is making it possible for Christians to participate profoundly in their faith. Existentialism has pressed theology into a regimen of intellectual roadwork destined to overcome some of the mental

51

obesity of the church and fit the church for the next round in its
contest for theological authenticity.

In the past theologies have sought help from philosophies which
could corroborate the substance of the faith. That generally was a
misalliance inspiring the question as to whether the faith had anything not already available in the philosophy. One's faith, it is now
realized, ought never be so intimate with philosophy that philosophy can claim paternity to the theology of the faith. Philosophy is
not the sire but the midwife of theology, delivering the insights
of faith into higher levels of understanding. A Christian, therefore,
does not seek a philosophy which already has the Christian substance within it. He seeks only "a philosophy of the Christian intention." (Roger Mehl)

Existentialism is such a philosophy. At a time when the category
of history has become paramount in the theology of the church,
existentialism is supplying an intellectual analysis which promises
to supplant substantialistic and naturalistic philosophies in use-
fulness to theological formulation. It has the added advantage of
being less intrusive than these more comprehensive philosophies,
having little to offer but an obstetric force upon the body of the
faith.

It will not be my intention in these pages to demonstrate how
theology can use existentialism apologetically. It is rather my
purpose to indicate how existentialism reflects our historical predicament in a secular and laicized way, how it exposes a kind of self-
awareness outside the church which is a wholesome spiritual expectation, and how this expectancy is there not for the church to
exploit, but as a kind of Macedonian invitation,—how it is there
for the church to address as rain speaks to parched ground when
low pressure areas form above it.

Part I, then, has the intention of showing how existentialism
illuminates what is being called existential history, and how it
clarifies the expectations implicit in what the Christian faith knows
as eschatological history. Existentialism records the imperious de-

mand of nature for a wholeness which nature does not itself supply. By that demand it arouses the historical consciousness of man, which is the quest for meaning. In that sense existential history is a mean between nature and God. (Chapter 2) Existentialism describes the ingredients in the composition of the self as freedom, shows how freedom makes history, how reason thereafter records that history. Existential freedom is thus at the base of what is known as the historical reason. (Chapter 3) Existentialism transcribes the human quest in terms so passionate and concerned as to border on a mysticism, differing from mysticism only by that constant falling short of ultimacy which is a characteristic of world history. This is not the ontological mysticism of the vertical ascent, but the horizontal, historical mysticism which constantly senses its upper limits in manifestations of restlessness and thirst. (Chapter 4) Even in its realization of the apparent absence of God from history, existentialism contributes to the lively hope in God's possible presence. (Chapter 5)

In the history of Christianity theology has often asked philosophy for bread and has received a stone. Today it will be enough if existentialism gives faith yeast.

CHAPTER
2

HISTORY BETWEEN NATURE AND GOD

EXISTENTIALISM has often been suspected of being a philosophy which is hostile toward science. That is a misapprehension. Existentialism is actually only concerned to give an exposition of a form of reality which is beyond the range of science's concern. That reality is history, where history is conceived as the realm in which man is struggling for his self-identity and searching for some clue to the ultimate meaning of his life. The object of science is nature, which is reality in so far as the question of ultimate meaning is not raised. The object of existentialism is history, which is reality in so far as the question of ultimate meaning is raised. The study of history brings a man no closer to God than the study of nature. The aim of this chapter, however, is twofold: first, to ask whether the question about reality can be raised in any ultimately meaningful way except as it is raised in the context of history; and second, to show how the sciences, while they do not deliberately ask the existential question, nevertheless unwittingly contribute to what is known as existential history.

When the scientist looks at nature he sees what Joseph Conrad calls "the balance of colossal forces." But he does not see what Joseph Conrad sees. It is not intended that he should. He does not ask the same questions; hence, he does not hear the same answers. The scientist lives to know. That is his vocation as a

scientist. Conrad, as any artist, knows to live. His vocation is closer
to the more comprehensive calling that constitutes one's integral
manhood. Scientists must weigh the forces of nature and math-
ematically compute the syntax in the relation between those
forces. The artist asks, however, where the fulcrum of the forces
lies and whether the forces are therefore humanly endurable. The
historical question is closer to the artist's. The historical spirit asks
for what is not given in the forces and for what is not computable
between the forces. Apart from an answer to his questions about
the paratactic spaces in the story of life, he has no assurance that
life is supported by a meaning adequate to its ongoing.

The historical spirit of man asks about the "soul" of the universe. This quest leads one to data about reality which are not
only unacceptable, but uninteresting and meaningless to the scientific spirit. The immensities of the universe are, to the scientific in
us, an invitation to travel; to the historical in us, an occasion for
loneliness. The apparently irreducible atoms of reality are, to the
scientist in us, an invitation to effect just one more fission; to the
historical in us, they are an occasion for insecurity. The forces of
the universe are to the scientific a source of power for locomotion;
to the historical, a source of emotional exhaustion until such time
as he finds rest. A scientist looking at a moving body knows it is
caught up in the force of the earth's rotation on its axis, knows
that the earth in turn is caught up in its own revolutions around
the sun, knows that this entire solar system is constantly slipping
off in the direction of the star Vega, knows that Vega itself is
gyrating from the impulses of the entire galactic system which in
turn gears its motions to the movements of the other galactic systems. But the historical spirit is not asking for some fulcrum in
space on which to rest all the vortices of the cosmos. It is asking
for the soul, the ultimate meaning, the ontological rest.

The traditional warfare between science and religion has been
at base the warfare between methods, the methods appropriate to
nature and the methods appropriate to history. The war continues

today, therefore, notwithstanding the widespread acceptance of a peaceful co-existence. This is so because the conditions of the peace have not radically affected the sources of the conflict. "The conflict between the natural sciences and religion," as Paul Tillich has said, "has been overcome in all important philosophies. The question as to whether Protestantism in particular has become stronger must be answered in the negative."[1] The conflict has originated out of the human unwillingness to embrace two different approaches to life. It has intensified whenever the operational distinction between these two approaches has not been kept quite clear. Heidegger has such a distinction in mind when he says, "Science today in all its circles is a technical, practical affair for the acquiring and use of knowledge. From science, as science, no awakening of the spirit can proceed. It needs such an awakening itself."[2]

These two approaches are requirements on the life of every man. In one sense, every man lives in order to know. He has a technical, practical way of acquiring knowledge for his use. In another sense, every man knows in order to live. If his spirit has been quickened, there are things he simply must know. To assume that because "truth is truth" all knowledge is alike is to court equivocation of the most perilous sort. For there are two distinct ways of knowing, productive of two different kinds of knowledge called nature and history. The bicephalous demand of knowledge rears its two heads in every single cognitive pursuit. The historical spirit requires the wisdom of the natural sciences in order to know, and the natural scientists require the vital spirit of the historical in order to live.

The warfare between science and religion is, therefore, not a warfare between two spaces which can be partitioned off but rather a warfare between dimensions of the human spirit which are organic to each other. A single individual is obliged at one and

[1] Paul Tillich, The Protestant Era, University of Chicago Press, 1948, p. 222.
[2] Martin Heidegger, Einführung in die Metaphysik, Tübingen, 1953, p. 37.

the same time to know in order to live and to live in order to know. When one demand of the human spirit is allowed to become exclusive of the other, there is interior disharmony. For instance, it would be a spiritual lie of comic proportions for one to live in today's world on the basis of a pre-Copernican science. Only open regard for the importance of living-to-know can keep free the spirit of knowing-to-live. Hence, history without science is sleepy.

However, science without history is sinister.[3] For if one were given the choice, he would find this life more viable on the basis of knowing-to-live than on any other basis. If these two strategies of life could be hierarchically arranged without violating their organicity, knowledge for living would appear to be more crucial for man than the living for knowledge. That is to say, the historical, meaning-seeking urges in man are ultimately more authentic than any other cognitive urges. The quest for a knowledge that supports life meaningfully is at the base of all living quests for knowledge. While the choice between Ptolemy and Copernicus is no longer a live option, there is little in modern, post-Copernican science that contributes to the *ultimate* support of life. For that reason, it is almost a matter of indifference to man's will to live whether he be Ptolemaic or Copernican in his astronomy. For instance, modern science has delayed death, but not everyone is grateful. Suicide is the testimony to that. Like an interstate commerce commission which declares you can travel farther now on the same ticket, science says you can now live longer. But occasionally someone respectfully returns the ticket as if the route were no longer traversible.

Is it not for this reason that the development of modern science is so crucial an event in the history of man? Not that science has obtained hierarchical superiority over religion and other historical disciplines, and that the relation should now be reversed—that

---

[3] I use the word "sinister" here in the sense of the German, *das Unheimliche*, the "not at home," or "strange," or "estranged." Cf. Heidegger, *ibid.*, pp. 115 and 116.

would be scholasticism. Actually the scientific and historico-religious spirits require each other to exist side by side and not one above the other. But rather, by their very popularity in life today, scientific interests have forced religious interests into a shade which is unconducive to their healthy development. By its phenomenal discoveries and through its beneficent by-products modern science has unwittingly won the heart of the world in much the same way as political paternalists secure themselves in office. Modern science by its spectacular feats has, like the muscular bodies of college boys in autumn, acquired prestige all out of proportion to its capacity to contribute to the human spirit. The effect of this is not that the *scientists* have gained control of the spirit of modern times, but that mankind has gradually allowed the passion to live in order to know to overpower its more authentic passion to know in order to live. If there no longer exists a warfare between religion and science, it is not because these disciplines have made a peace. Nor is it because science has said religion is defunct. Scientists know that is not for the sciences to say. It is because the popularity of the scientific spirit, only one operation of the total human personality, has contributed to the general sense of the uselessness of religion. The spirit of living to know thus ironically undercuts the very knowledge that supports life. The lover who is bent upon unveiling the goddess of love should therefore be prepared for the collapse of his beloved.[4]

I. THE FREEDOM IN THINGS

When Joseph Conrad spoke of nature as a colossal force, he was beholding the wing of a butterfly. The flux of nature is as contorted in the wing of a butterfly as in the whirl of planets, and its vortex as deep. Where lies the fulcrum and does it support life? "To be or not to be"—is that the question? Only if you footnote

---

[4] Reference to a story from Novalis cited by Wilhelm Dilthey in "Einleitung in die Geisteswissenschaften," *Gesammelte Schriften*, Leipzig and Berlin, 1914, Vol. I, p. 405.

that question with the drama and panic of the inner life out of which it is asked.

The scientist cannot answer this question as a scientist. Some scientists continue to regard the question as meaningless so long as it remains scientifically inaccessible. To erect that sentiment as dogma, however, would be the final capitulation of all life to but one perspective on life. It is, therefore, reassuring to discover in the most deliberately scientific of the philosophies today a revision of this dogma to the effect that what is not scientifically verifiable simply is not *scientifically* meaningful.[1]

In order to live with equanimity in the presence of things one must know their soul. The scientist is less apt to ask what things are than what they do. Therefore, science feeds the technological spirit of the times more than it does the historical spirit.[2] Victor Hugo, however, was no less vulnerable than Gladstone in his relation to science. When Gladstone had heard Faraday explain a new scientific discovery, he responded, "But after all, what use is it?" When Hugo had heard Arago, the French astronomer, describe an astral phenomenon, he responded, "But Monsieur Arago, what is the *soul* of a comet?" The findings of science do lend themselves to technological uses, it is true, even though the motivations of science are not primarily technological. But it is unfair to ask the scientist the historical question, for this question arises in the dimension of the human spirit which the scientists are not vocationally required or even allowed to employ. The question about the soul of things, about the fulcrum of the balance of nature, is the quest for wholeness in reality, the historical question. Now there is a slight sense in which the scientist asks this question, too. Gestalt psychology has accentuated the importance to science of the structure in objects, and logical positivism, the philosophy of

[1] Herbert Feigl, "Scientific Method without Metaphysical Presuppositions," *Philosophical Studies*, V, Part II, February, 1954, p. 20. Cf. the correlation of skepticism and faith in Ludwig Wittgenstein, inspired by David Hume.

[2] Cf. Heidegger, *Holzwege*, Frankfurt, 1950, p. 70, where he lists as the three characteristics of science today exactitude, research, and production.

the sciences, has stressed the structure in the language about reality which is really the structure of the relation between objects. Even prior to these developments in modern science, the scientist was undergoing a kind of aesthetic experience in the intuition which sprang from his experiments. "It suddenly flashed upon me" is the testimony of almost every discoverer among the scientists, which is to say, "the whole project came to a focus." But this is not the wholeness about which the historical spirit is concerned. "Give me a tooth and I will reconstruct the whole animal," cried Cuvier. But he could not arrive at the wholeness of the animal which is its meaning, its ontological rest, the fulcrum which balances the forces in the butterfly's wing. Cavendish, who could weigh the world, could never spell Atlas at shouldering the world. A contemporary physicist is more comparable to a physician than to a watchmaker. He is concerned with the whole of life more than with its parts. Historically viewed, however, what he draws into the sphere of his calculations is at last only a very large part of the whole and not the wholeness, for he does not perceive the soul in things, their meaning, the *uni*verse.

The most important contemporary exception to this claim is found in the scientific metaphysics of Alfred North Whitehead and in the theological methodologies that derive from his system.[3] Whitehead finds in the contemporary science of mathematics the possibility for doing what both the Stoics and the Hegelians have done in the past but on the basis of now discredited sciences. For both the Stoics and Hegel it was possible to break into the universe at any point and have the wholeness of things. The Stoics could do this on the basis of what they called "seeds of the reason" immanent in all reality, the conviction being that the wholeness of the universe is implicit in any part as the wholeness of the plant is

[3] E.g., Henry Nelson Wieman, Daniel Day Williams, Bernard Meland, Bernard Loomer, Harold A. Bosley, and in some respects Nels F. S. Ferré. Cf. L. S. Thornton in England. *Vide* Carl G. Fjellmann, *Process Theology*, unpublished doctoral dissertation, Drew University, Madison, N. J., 1955.

implicit in the seed. Hegel could do the same on the basis that all reality is the historical unfolding of a basic oneness in reality. Whitehead finds it possible for the whole to be in every part on the basis of a theory of the continuum of experience in which all elements of reality may be comprehended in any event in reality. "The full universe disclosed for every variety of experience is a universe in which every detail enters into its proper relationship with the immediate occasion."[4] For these three systems, therefore, it is impossible to use the word "knowledge" equivocally. One has either ignorance or knowledge. He cannot have in one and the same moment historical ignorance and scientific knowledge or vice versa. Hence, religious, metaphysical, historical knowledge claims the same status as knowledge as does scientific knowledge, and to the ears of the contemporary man leading the life of stagedoor Johnny to the sciences this word has a strangely wooing effect.

Whitehead's metaphysics, however, is essentially no more scientific than the metaphysics of the Stoics and Hegelians. His theory of how the wholeness of reality can be in every part is not derived from his scientific method any more than Newton's exegesis of the Book of Daniel was derived from his law of gravitation. The misleading thing is that his metaphysical conjecture, associated as it is with his reputation as a scientist, is prone to win adherence as much on the strength of the current prestige of the sciences as on the intrinsic merit of his metaphysics.

Two things are in the main wrong with Whitehead's scheme. The lesser evil is that he fuses with his science a metaphysical dogma that says order is at the base of the universe. It is his conviction that the dogma need not be dogmatically held because science, he believes, could not proceed without the postulate of cosmic order. And obviously science is proceeding. He applauds the "rationalism of the middle ages" which, conserving the concept of order at the base of things, kept alive the theoretical possibility of

[4] Alfred North Whitehead, *Science in the Modern World*, Mentor, 1948, p. 27.

an experimental science even while organized religion, which had sponsored the faith in order, retarded scientific practice. But Whitehead's dogma is not shared by working scientists. An experimental science requires no metaphysical presuppositions. The successful functioning of a science may even be as dependent upon skepticism as the success of a religion is dependent upon faith. In any case, as long as one scientist can make verifiable judgments about the conduct of nature without the benefit of the dogma of an order behind it, Whitehead is wrong. The apparent orderliness of the universe that turns up in scientific laws can as readily be explained on the basis of statistical averages and probability quotients as on the basis of orderly laws in the nature of things. The regularity in the described processes of nature is attributable as well to the infinite number of elements at play in observed reality to which statistical averages pertain, as to an *a priori* orderliness in things. The greater the number of indeterminate realities under observation, the greater is the aspect of their stability and regularity in the findings of the observer. The scientist has at last to do not primarily with his laws, but with the indeterminable minutiae of reality out of which his laws are delineated.[5]

The greater evil in Whitehead's metaphysic of order is that if the scientist took it seriously, he would no longer be a beholder of the total spectacle of nature. He would deal in the order of nature alone and would miss whatever else was there—perchance the disorder. He would study cancer for the orderly laws in the pathology of the development of cancerous cells and miss what the poet Rilke

[5] Cf. Feigl, *op. cit.*, p. 19: "One would wish to know what the rationalists have to say on the geometrical relation of electric and magnetic field vectors —this basic asymmetry in our universe should certainly shatter one's faith in a priori discernible laws of nature." Cf. also p. 21: "What type and degree of uniformity must the universe possess in order to be successfully predictable by means of the inductive and hypothetico-deductive procedures of modern science? I think the answer to this question is very obvious. The universe must have precisely the type and degree of uniformity which the successfully confirmed laws and theories ascribe to it (or rather, to some of its aspects)."

calls, "the cracks in things"[6] which make a cancer possible, and by that same token he would miss the cracks in things which make a cancer endurable.

Science does reality an injustice when on the basis of its empirical data it extrapolates a world view to which it subsequently subjugates its scientific method. The most important philosophical event behind the rise of modern science has been the bifurcation of thought from extension through the philosophy of Descartes. From that moment on nature has been allowed to speak for itself. It is not required to confess in conformity to the mentalistic prejudices of its interrogator, the human spirit. The event second in importance to this has been the Humean skepticism about causes, cropping up today in the scientifically sponsored judgment regarding nature as acausal. Acausality, however, is not a dogmatic metaphysical alternative to causality, but a methodological suspension of the old judgment that every effect is preceded by a cause so that when cause-effect sequences are once perceived, you can capture the wholeness of nature in a law. The Humean skepticism about law is of a piece with the Cartesian separation of nature from the human mind. The net result for science is a concept of micro-physical freedom which deals with "atoms" as it sees them and, like Democritus, lets the void beneath be. It does not fill the void with metaphysical inferences which are closer to the scientist's mind than to the nature of things. When the scientist tells his story of the universe, there are prolonged and profound silences, gaps in the story corresponding to the cracks in things. The whole story, the story of nature as a universe, therefore, is not told until the void has spoken and the cracks are filled.

II. THE FEAR IN FREEDOM

The real "*faux-pas*" in the Cartesian bifurcation of thought and extension has not been the separation of the mental from the material, but the separation of man from nature. The separation

[6] *Letters*, Norton, Vol. 2, p. 149.

of the mental from the natural has fostered a wholesome objectivity in science, but the separation of man from nature has allowed the human approach to reality to default in the writing of the whole story of the universe. It has not taken account of what happens in the human spirit when the objectivities of nature are found to be riddled with holes, the filling of which is basic to a sense of support in life. German phenomenology, stemming from Descartes through Husserl, has persistently required the sciences to deal with the facts themselves but has refused to deal with what does not appear. This is fine for the scientist *qua* scientist, but what of the scientist *qua* man? What shall he do with the sense of panic in his spirit when he peeks into nature and senses the intangible, invisible abyss through the cracks in things? He may pull himself together and re-focus his eyes upon the object. It is the object with which the scientist deals most efficiently. As Karl Jaspers has said, "Science is conscious that it would cease to exist if it did not have an object."[1] But what of the connection between objects, the web of life that supports all life?

Here French existentialism prefers Pascal to Descartes, without, of course, depreciating Descartes. Pascal found that the evidence in nature required the scientist to concern himself with another kind of reality—with history. That is, the new reflection upon nature forced upon one conclusions more about oneself than about the objective world of nature, as in the case of Prince Myshkin in Dostoevsky's *The Idiot*, who, watching a waterfall in Switzerland and smelling the resinous pine trees, "was sometimes overcome with great restlessness."

The new science first contributed to existential history in western culture through evoking the *esprit de finesse* of Pascal.

> This is our true state, this is what makes us incapable of certain knowledge and of absolute ignorance. We sail within a vast sphere, ever drifting in uncertainty, driven

[1] *Philosophie*, 2nd unchanged edition, Berlin-Göttingen-Heidelberg, 1948, p. 273.

from end to end. When we think to attach ourselves to any point and to fasten to it, it wavers and leaves us, and if we follow it, it eludes our grasp, slips past us and vanishes forever. Nothing stays for us; this is our natural condition and yet most contrary to our inclination. We burn with desire to find solid ground and an ultimate sure foundation whereon to build a tower reaching to the infinite, but our whole groundwork cracks and the earth opens to abysses.[2]

The scientist *qua* scientist must not allow himself to be diverted from the laboratory investigation of nature by these question marks which his inner spirit poises over the cracks in things. He must, if necessary, enforce his concentration on the object as Emil du-Bois-Reymond did at the end of his treatise on *The Limitations of Natural Science*. He must fill these gaps with the word *ignorabimus* and hold himself to what he can know. But on his bed at night he will be pursued by the vision of what he *qua* scientist cannot know, the consciousness in his spirit which John Donne expressed (as previously quoted) upon entering into the first phases of modern science, "Tis all in peeces, all cohaerence gone." Can he then be satisfied to ignore completely what he must know if he is to live? Pascal knew what contemporary science has now begun to make more widely and poignantly patent: that natural science is independent of man and of the human will and that its knowledge is determined by the object, by the facts in things.[3] He also knew that to abandon the quest for knowledge at the level of the natural sciences would be to end one's investigation of the natural at the level of the "artificial." There is an "original" being in nature which appears to the scientist only as an absence, only as "a crack in the groundwork." One cannot come by the knowledge of this original element in nature by holding nature off at arm's length, but only by entering into a concerned personal relation with it, which is history. The scientist *qua* scientist deliberately suspends the predicament which is his existential history. Yet it is through

[2] Pascal, *Pensées*, fragment 72. Cf. also fragment 205.
[3] *Ibid.*, fragment 555.

this history that the truth about nature seems at last to shine. For man is "a mean between everything and nothing," as Pascal has said. It is through his history that one may arrive at a knowledge of the whole.[4]

What, then, may man discover when he brings himself into relation to nature? He may discover "the cracks in things." He may discover that these cracks witness to the freedom in things. The witness to this freedom may be the revelation of an abyss into which one falls unless there be an unanticipated support. He may see the "balance of colossal forces" as an unsteady teetering which threatens his very being unless there be a reliable fulcrum which does not yet appear. He may see all life as a vast oceanic expanse on which nothing can leave a record. He may see nature as "formidably insecure," "the formidable work of the Seven Days into which mankind seems to have blundered unbidden or else decoyed."[5] He may see life as a rusted-out tramp in a storm or a three-master in a calm and he will have the constant inclination to leap, "a despairing desire to escape." An abyss will be in his wake, a luminous immensity ahead, and a pitiless sky above. He may dream of a "safe universe," or he may leap from the ship. If he leaps, he may discover that simply thrashing about holds him up, but he will nevertheless be haunted by the unendurable realization that all his ills root back in one fault: "I jumped."[6]

This analysis of the sinister aspect of nature taken from the works of Joseph Conrad seems to be remarkably in continuity with Pascal. Its motifs recur today in the poetry of Rilke and in the philosophy of the existentialists. It is based on the conviction that nature has lessons which the scientists do not read from it, but which are nonetheless there. These lessons pertain to the kind of being a man discovers in himself when he relates himself to nature quite concretely. No human discipline brings man closer to the

[4] *Ibid.*, fragment 72.
[5] Joseph Conrad, *The Shadow Line*, Doubleday, p. 97.
[6] *Lord Jim*, Modern Library, pp. 11, 214, 133.

concrete elements in nature than the natural sciences. This is their importance to the wholeness of man's life. They save man from the abstract and fictional that is so easily created out of the mind of a life unengaged by nude reality. The alliance with the concrete makes it forever impossible for one to repeat the vapid phrases that marked the last century's concessions to what it believed to be the message of science to man. That "what impresses us about nature is its solidity" can no longer be repeated from the Henry Drummonds. Wordsworth is closer to the latest word from science when he labels nature *insolido*, and then goes off in search of a creed that can make him less "forlorn." It is a judgment from the nineteenth century that "in earlier times man received his dogmas from councils, today from academies of science." (Taine) But the academies of science, when they are visited by living men who hear about "the cracks in things" and feel their own uncertain life, will send men off in wistfulness for a clue from the void that can still the turbulence of nature—that gambler which "wins every toss." (Conrad)

It is at this point that Whitehead's suggestions about religion and science leave something to be desired. One singles out Whitehead because of his tremendous authority on this matter today. It is a long and rewarding step from White's *Warfare of Science with Theology* (1896) to Whitehead's *Science and the Modern World* (1925). White sought to free science from religion and became the president of a university founded on just such a policy of non-interference. Whitehead has sought to save science for religion and religion for science, an interaction which one would suppose quite basic to a *uni*versity.

But Whitehead's philosophy is deficient in anthropology and therefore in history. His view of the relation between science and religion is a piecing together of the findings of two diverse disciplines without passing them through that "mean between everything and nothing" which is man. Whitehead substitutes abstract mathematical syntax for concrete existential relation. He expresses the jarring asymmetry in nature more as a musical score than as a tune one sings, feeling the dissonance through his very being. Hence, while he escapes the sentimentality toward nature which characterized romanticism, he does not enter into the sinister aspects of nature which are revealed when sensitive men place themselves in relation to the newly understood universe.

One evidence of this can be seen in his interpretation of Greek tragedy. In the Greek notion of fate Whitehead finds the real origin of modern science, for the meaning of fate articulates the Greek sense for order in the universe. What Whitehead neglects to observe is the psychological reaction of the Greek man to his involvement in fate, a reaction in which the man is made more conscious of himself, his weakness and his guilt, and of the sinister quality of existence in which he feels quite strange, than he is of order. Whitehead rarely if ever notices the pre-Socratic philosophical parallels to the fate of the Greek tragedy which are more taken up with the numinous quality of the power of fate than with its rational and aesthetic orderliness. There are cracks in the orderliness of being through which man sees the possibility of powerfully unpredictable impulses toward himself. Their presence evokes in him unquenchably heroic instincts to leap against his fate.

These are the terrifying freedoms in nature. They are the freedoms to which Whitehead seems as oblivious as was Lucretius in his "artificial" account of *The Nature of Things.* The fear of nature is based not upon one's ignorance of nature, as Lucretius seemed to suggest it is, but upon one's knowledge of himself in the face of nature. One cannot, therefore, quiet this fear of a man who faces the abyss of reality by telling him nature carries its own explanation, as Lucretius seemed to do, for he is not now concerned alone with nature. He is concerned with himself in relation to nature and he is conscious of falling through the spaces in its groundwork. He may sometime end his fall, abruptly finding himself stuck in life as in a "soft and sticky mud-bank," and when he finds he cannot move his legs, he may then come to himself.[7] But that will happen only if, when he considers the heavens, he also asks himself, "What is man?" (Psalm 8)

Karl Heim's contribution to the solution of this problem suffers from the same neglect as Whitehead's, the neglect of man as the mean between nature and God. While Whitehead uses his own religious understanding to support with piety a kind of mysticism in his mathematical metaphysics, Heim uses his own understanding of science to support the articles of the Christian faith. This was not his intention at the outset. As far back as 1904 in his *Weltbild der Zukunft* and more clearly in his essay, "Der gegenwärtige Stand der Debatte zwischen. Theologie und Naturwissenschaft,"[8] he was claiming what he reasserts in his current trilogy on Christianity and science.[9] The Christian apologetic, he insisted, must be offensive and not defensive. But when the three elements in his apologetic method are summed up, I believe one must say he has related Christianity to science defensively.

The elements involved in Heim's apologetic are threefold. First is his policy of withdrawal. Christianity must determine what its invulnerable beliefs are and stay within them. This apparently protective attitude he does not construe as a defensive move, however. It is rather the securing of one's supply lines as the prelude to attack. The second element is his policy of attack. This element is much more obvious in his other writings than in his writings about science, for he is exceedingly cautious in these earlier writings lest he alienate the scientist. The best attack upon science, he believes, is to adopt the position of the scientist in so far as that

---

[7] *Ibid.*, p. 253. It should not be concluded from my comments about Whitehead that his philosophy contains no appreciation of the tragic element in life. For a balanced appraisal of his position *see* Lee Underhill, *The Problem of Evil in the Philosophy of Alfred North Whitehead*, unpublished doctoral dissertation, Drew University, Madison, N. J., 1957.

[8] *Theologische Studien und Kritiken*, 1908, pp. 402-29.

[9] *Christian Faith and Natural Science, The Transformation of the Scientific World View*, and the as yet untranslated *Weltschöpfung und Weltende*.

is possible without vulgarizing faith. Scientific truth becomes a valuable ally in the destruction of false faith and false elements in true faith. For instance, materialism as a faith is no longer easily held when it is known what contemporary science understands about the constitution of matter.[10] The third element in Heim's apologetic is the construction of a world-view. Apologists ought to have an alternative ready for their antagonists when the position they have attacked is rendered untenable. It is only moral, if one's warfare makes refugees of people, that one offer them a habitable home, an alternate world-view.

Somewhere in the movement from the second to the third element, however, Heim's strategy seems to weaken. There is the recurrent inference in his writings that when a false position is discredited, Christian faith is thereby established as truth and that the sole remaining step is to adopt the new truth. In the case of the scientist this seems to be quite easy because scientific results can be manipulated to corroborate the Christian faith at so many points.

Two elements are overlooked here, however. First, interest in the Christian faith as truth is not aroused simply by the loss of some supposed truth. One has first to feel that loss as a loss of his very self. Only if he is, in some sense, his ideas does the denial to him of his ideas come as a serious loss. Secondly, the acceptability of an alternative truth is not contingent upon that truth's scientific certification but upon the capacity of that truth to authenticate one's life, to lift him beyond the predicament which is his existential history.

III. FREEDOM FROM FEAR

Nature, when it is engaged, can pitch man into dry-mouthed fear over the status of being, as manifested in himself. This fear is the human reaction to the looseness in nature, its cracks, its mo-

[10] See The Transformation of the Scientific World View, S. C. M. Press, 1953, pp. 62-3.

bility, its evanescence and viscosity—its contingency. This is not a fear born of ignorance, though it is not withheld from the ignorant. On the contrary, it is a fear elicited by the candid and objective data of the experimental sciences when that data is entered into by living men. Nor is it an emotional fear of the sort one contracts out of "failure of nerve." It is an ontological fear which contributes, like the restless needle of a compass, to the total direction of a man's life, to the project which is his "courage to be."

Corresponding to the freedom in nature which evokes man's fear is the historical freedom which anticipates the dissolution of this fear. Lucretius attempted to eradicate the failure of nerve from ancient Rome by a technological point of view but fear persisted. Julian Huxley announced on the eve of the birth of the age of anxiety that science had exorcised all fears. The impressive fact of our time is that the deeper science probes into the heart of reality, the more it contributes to the sense of the sinister in life. There is a freedom in man, however, to adopt an attitude toward things which replaces fear with an understanding of the meaning behind things. This is the attitude which supplements the facts of nature with the acts of faith—acts which respond affirmatively to the possibility that "the cracks in things" are apertures through which the essence of a faithful reality at the ground of things shines through.

There is no scientific warrant for such an act of faith. The predicament which science reveals to the life of man is not itself scientifically soluble. But surely the sciences will not begrudge to man non-scientific solutions to matters which science suggests and yet is unable to address itself. Were it to deny this act to man, it would be filling the cracks in nature. Actually, it is vocationally equipped only to arouse a consciousness of them. It would be usurping under a single attitude all the responsibilities of the personality. In such an attempt science would not be simply limited; it would be wrong.

Indeed, religion has quaked too long in the presence of the

scientific demand for exactitude. To require all the relations of life to come under the test of exactitude breeds greater confusion than to accept guidance from the inexact. In fact, the ambiguous and unknowable character of that sphere of reality which remains after science has made its investigations is a kind of invitation to faith. As Gabriel Marcel has said, "Faith (and thence, spirituality) is only possible if metaphysical doubt is in some way imposed on the mind by the nature—in itself indeterminable—of the object."[1] The acts of science are based on the action of man in his separation from reality—his inquiry into, his manipulation of, his recording of the facts as they appear. But what if man sees *himself* in relation to reality as observed? What if his relation to nature awakens in him the dimension of an existential history? Here the person becomes the mediator between reality and whatever is possibly at the ground of reality. Man becomes the "mean between everything and nothing."

Science cannot act as science in the realm of possibility, but religion can act only in this realm, for this is the realm of freedom and of spirit. The realm of existential history is a realm where only acts of faith can be committed. An act of faith, however, is not an act of self-blinding to factual realities. It is an act which chooses enlightenment, an act that constitutes man free without abridging freedom. Thought first discovered its freedom in its movement from metaphorical meanings to literal meanings. That was the movement of science. Thought now confirms and constitutes its freedom in the movement from the literal to the higher metaphorical. That is the movement of history. Existential history suggests that man may choose to know himself in the face of the possible faithfulness at the ground of being.

Existential history, however, is a movement in possibility, not in necessity. That is why freedom and history are synonyms while nature and history are only correlates. Jacob Boehme and Jean-Paul Sartre, for instance, have drawn identical conclusions about

[1] *Metaphysical Journal*, Regnery, 1952, p. 96.

nature. When Roquentin in the novel *Nausea* contemplates the root of a chestnut tree, he sees it shimmer and fade in evanescence. Nature lacks solidity. There is no firm standing ground there. Hence, Sartre's hero feels sick with nature, and plunges himself into existential history which has no ultimate answers yet deplores that man must live in such a world. Boehme, on the other hand, contemplates nature in a polished pewter dish and observes that "nature is only motion, a restless search for satisfaction which cannot be found in itself." But where Sartre settles for existential history, which is the sense of the irreducible nothingness in things, Boehme concludes that "the abyss of nature and creation is God himself." Man can stand in nature if he can believe that God is at its ground. Either conclusion is a possibility. To live in existential history is to know a man is free for either nothingness or God. That means that the "order of nature" can be like an "order of worship." Its intention is to carry you beyond itself toward the mystery which is the power of God's being.

The action of Galileo in affirming the law of inertia is based upon what Galileo supposed was fact. (It is of no great consequence to my point here or even to the subsequent history of science that his facts were not entirely true.) The decision of Luther to live by faith alone was no less authentic than Galileo's for being less factual or necessary or exact. The human spirit simply cannot survive on the basis of answers to answerable questions alone. It must risk resolving itself about some unanswerable questions. The rarest capacity of the human spirit is this freedom and with the risk there comes the responsibility for holding by an act of resolution a truth of being which otherwise could escape the mind of man for dangerously protracted intervals. Galileo refused to die for what he knew to be the truth because he knew it as a fact, and the truth of facts will sooner or later get around to everyone. Giordano Bruno died for what he held as truth because he knew it as a faith, and the truth of faith maintains itself through the medium of its believers and their resolute witness.[2]

This is not to suggest that the acts of faith are performed *in vacuo* as arbitrary and groundless. There are "the cracks in things." But where the scientist may hear nothing and where the man engaged by nature may sense his possible nothingness, God has his own possibility. Herein lies the meaning of miracle in Christianity. In the New Testament, miracle is always the sign that God is doing something, that God is present in power. Quite obviously, a miracle is not a fact of nature or else it would contribute to the body of knowledge that sooner or later gets around to everyone. It is rather a crack in nature, an absence which man is free to interpret as God's presence. Here one must prefer Calvin to Hegel. For Hegel, miracles were "unnatural" because they were "the deepest crack" in nature,[3] and he rejected them. For Calvin miracles were indeed a rent in nature deliberately devised by God to keep man reminded that the spaces between things were filled not by mechanical joints but by God's own faithful will.[4] These cracks in nature called miracle are the answer to man's fear of what lies beyond nature and the possibility of his life of trust within nature. But the miracle is maltreated when one focuses his will to know upon the event and makes of it an object, for in that moment two things go wrong. First, he disregards the crack in nature which is his access to the ground of being. And second, he steps outside the relationship which binds him to the event, which is his personal freedom to choose its meaning for himself. Hence, either the rationalistic defense of miracles or the rationalistic attack upon miracles nullifies the integral validity of the miracle. Miracle at one and the same time draws upon man's deepest desires to leap and provides the hope of a ground beyond nature's *insolido* on which to land. "Hope is only possible in a world where there is room for

[2] Karl Jaspers, *Perennial Scope of Philosophy*, Philosophical Library, 1949, pp. 4, 5.
[3] *Hegels Theologische Jugendschriften*, edited by Nohl, Tübingen, 1907, p. 339.
[4] John Calvin, *The Institutes of the Christian Religion*, Book I, chap. xvi, iii.

miracles." (Marcel)[5] The modern sciences have quite unintentionally inspired the conjecture that there may be room—in the cracks in things. What fills the cracks is not within the method of science to determine. If the light is an eternal light, it cannot be looked upon directly, as science looks. One sees its ray subdued and indistinct, said Gregory the Great, as sunbeams passing through a chink in a darkened room.[6]

But how, without the help of science, can one be certain when some crack in nature called a miracle is a valid support in reality and not a mere projection of the human desire? We cannot. At least we cannot be certain in the dimension of the spirit that lives in order to know. How then does one deal with another who does not see the miracle? Scarcely by appealing to the side of his nature which by its very hyperactivity is already contributing to the spiritual blindness. The side of one's nature which knows in order to live must come into play. The historical dimension must be activated to interpret his life and pin his destiny upon the glimmer from that crack in nature. The side of his being which lives in order to know will thereupon initiate an endless attack, denying him this supportive truth with the call to intellectual responsibility and the promise of some more well supported truth. Luther expressed this attack as *Anfechtung*, the temptation not to trust. Indeed, this is the necessary and indispensable warfare between science and religion which is located within the human spirit. It becomes self-destructive and fatal to faith only when one side of the dialogue utterly engulfs the other—only when the religious spirit fossilizes against the possibility of revision, losing its spiritual freedom, or when the scientific spirit filibusters man's life beyond the deadline for authentic resolution.

Two things, however, can yet be said for the miracle. For one thing the act by which a man accepts it is not a lower act of man for being less certain, that is, less scientific. The confidence won by sensitivity to a wholeness supportive of the "peeces" of nature

[5] Marcel, *Being and Having*, Dacre Press, 1949, p. 75.
[6] *Morals*, V, 52.

is the wager on which man stakes his hope that nature does not win in every toss. The question to ask of a miracle, then, is not "Can you be certain of it?" but "Can you *be* without it?"

In the second place, one ought never let his will to know erase his memory of the story that supports his will to live. The criterion of a miracle is not just any old crack in nature. Miracle is believed to have taken place when a crack in things becomes the instrument for revealing the wholeness underneath. When the groundwork of life gapes open and one stares into the "infinite abyss," if the abyss is filled by God himself, a miracle has occurred.[7] Surely that is what Edwin Muir must mean in *One Foot in Eden* when he says quite cryptically, "There is no trust but in the miracle." Miracle is the crack in things through which the fullness of God appears, in whom all things cohere and upon whom at last all radically contingent reality rests.[8] The question one really wants answered about miracle, then, is not "Could it have happened?" but "Was God present?" Belief enters when other beliefs which constitute one's being are fractured by the encounter with life. This is what Ortega calls the orthopedic character of beliefs.[9] To be sure, one ought never to live so securely that his beliefs remain exempt from fracture. Science and the will to know will keep that possibility alive. At the same time one ought never permit himself to lose the sense of gratitude he felt when his wounds were once so inexplicably healed.

---

[7] Pascal, *Pensées*, fragment 425.

[8] See Rudolf Bultmann's essay, "Zur Frage des Wunders," in his *Glauben und Verstehen*, Tübingen, 1933, Vol. I, pp. 214ff. Bultmann identifies *Wunder* with the miracle which reveals God and *Mirakel* with assumed irregularities in nature having no revelatory significance. Some of his critics think that his Newtonian orientation to nature seems to require him to deny the cracks in things and therefore any cosmological corollary to miracle. That is not true. He only denies that the cracks are the miracles.

[9] *Idées et Croyances*, Paris 1945, translation from the Spanish, p. 34. *See also* David C. White, *The Historical Reason in the Thought of Jose Ortega y Gasset*, unpublished doctoral dissertation, Drew University, Madison, N. J., 1958.

CHAPTER

3

FREEDOM AND
THE HISTORICAL REASON

THE human reason can function within the limits accepted by the scientific method. When it does, however, it is quite a different instrument from the reason which chooses history as its context. History is human life in the exercise and expression of its freedom. Historical thinking, therefore, is based upon an activity of human life more original than thinking. That is why an understanding of the historical character of reality and of the operation of the human reason owes more to the word "freedom" than to any other word.

Nothing from the lips of philosophers and theologians is more productive of what the Frenchman, Parain, has called "the giddy sensation of the inexactitude of speech" than the word "freedom." Theology's ambiguous exposition of freedom can largely be attributed to the ill-fitting instruments of definition it has had at hand. Theologians have generally turned to philosophy for the tools of definition. The liability in this alliance has been that philosophy designs its words to fit its own concerns. Because philosophy's concerns have not always been the same as theology's concerns, its definitions have not always been theologically ample. The great bulk of philosophy from Democritus to Descartes has been preoccupied with the problem of nature. Its discussions of freedom have been drawn into the orbit of nature.

79

The depths of the experience of freedom are not probed, however, until it is discussed as a synonym of history. It is an intellectual event of major importance that theology is now turning for its definition of freedom to existentialism. In existentialism, philosophical and theological concerns have come together in a way unprecedented in western thought. The reason is that existentialism and theology alike are preoccupied with the question of history.

In the Greek tradition, for instance, philosophy defined man's problem as deliverance from the realm of necessity, which it called nature. Plato outlined a solution in a philosophy which built a case for human independence from nature. He called this independence freedom. Freedom was achievable by rational affiliation with an abstract realm of essences which were themselves beyond and independent of nature. Only the human body was considered a victim of nature's necessity. The human reason, transcendent of the body, was free from nature.

The reason, however, was not in itself free. To be rational was instinctively to know the essences—the true and the good. Nor was the will free, for it was the necessity of the will automatically to do what the reason knew. That is why in the realm of morals "to prefer evil to good is not in human nature." (*Protagoras* 758 C) Man does no evil voluntarily. Sin stems from an ignorance for which one is not culpable. The body, a foreign agent, subverts the reason. Knowledge is virtue. (*Gorgias* 468, *Timaeus* 86, *Laws* V, 731) Greek philosophy, while it understood that man was free from doing what comes naturally, nevertheless delivered human nature into another kind of necessity, the necessity for doing what comes rationally. Escape from the causes of nature was achieved by subjection to the necessitarian logic of essences.

To be just to the lively sense of freedom in men, the Greeks devised a concept of "free choice." In the last analysis, however, "free choice" meant simply the consciousness of alternate ways of doing what it is finally necessary to do. Free choice, the prisoner of reason, "mimics freedom by pacing round and round in his cell." (Helmut Kuhn)

In the German tradition man's problem was not so much how to escape from nature as how to safeguard moral responsibility. Motivated by this shift in the problem, Immanuel Kant took it upon himself to by-pass the thousand-year-old philosophical contradiction which defined freedom as rational determinism. The *will* is free, Kant said. It is possible for a man to say either "yes" or "no" to what he knows to be the good, the right, and the true, for reason is shot through with will. Descartes had hinted at this. When man acted in his ignorance, Descartes did not blame the body for disfiguring the reason, as Plato did. He blamed the will for acting in the absence of a clear idea. This was the only basis on which it seemed possible, according to Kant, to keep morality alive. Unless one is free to choose either good or evil, he is not responsible, and neither merit nor guilt attaches to his choice. Freedom makes man accountable and makes either merit or guilt imputable.

Further to enhance this responsible moral freedom Kant transplanted the heaven of ethical ideals, with its hierarchical dominion over man, into the human reason. Man, then, could be his own law-giver. Thus, in the eighteenth century autonomy became "inseparably connected" with freedom.[1] Autonomy did not mean antinomianism or anarchy, for the law within is as universal and irrevocable as if it were the law above. Autonomy simply avoided the causal and necessitarian implications in an alliance with either nature or a realm of essences. The law is not the cause, of which moral living is the inescapable effect. It is possible for man to obey or disobey it. One ought to note, however, that the law of good, before which the will decides, is as rational for Kant as it is for Plato. The good is the rational. To that extent Plato survives in Kant. The major difference is that for Kant the will, though obliged by the rational, is not compelled by it. Freedom of the

[1] *The Metaphysics of Ethics*, Appleton, 1938, p. 72.

will as voluntaristic indeterminism thereby supplanted philosophy's long-standing definition of freedom as rational determinism.

The Kantian philosophy of freedom is the confluence of two intellectual streams. Greek philosophy's concern for the superiority of the rational over the natural merges with Medieval Europe's Romano-Germanic concern for moral responsibility. The Christian freedomists, whose major theological concerns were merit and guilt—Pelagius, Thomas Aquinas, Erasmus, and the seventeenth-century Jesuits—are in Kant's philosophical family tree as truly as Plato, Aristotle, and the Stoics, whose philosophical concern was the rational. The twin requirements of the Kantian moral philosophy were rational insight into moral truth and the deliberate decision of the will.

Another intellectual stream in Western thought, however, is represented by Augustine, the voluntarists of the fourteenth century, the Reformers, and the Jansenists. No matter how dependent this stream may have been upon Graeco-Roman thinking, when it came to problems involving freedom it found this line too slack to hold the Christian faith. How talk of rational insight into human destiny when the sovereign of history is the hidden God who reveals himself at will? How talk of moral responsibility in a man whose entire life is under the fate of sin and whose Christian hope is a destiny that lies beyond history, a destiny whose operation is so free it is unconditioned by the acts of man? The predestinarian categories of the Augustinian tradition clash with both the rationalistic and the moralistic categories of the Greek and Roman traditions. The fact that contemporary theology is built upon this uneven tripod of traditions surely helps to account for "the giddy sensation" in the contemporary use of the word "freedom."

I. HISTORY AS FUTURE

Meanwhile, a species of philosophy has developed which is rapidly breaking up these unsteady historical alternatives and retooling the instruments for defining freedom. It is a cluster of vitalisms, pragmatisms, and existentialisms. Despite important differences among these new philosophies, they agree on two points: first, that "existence precedes essence"; second, that this precedence is the rudiment of freedom. Living is given priority over thinking. The whole of one's life, which is history, is given priority over that partial function of life which is reason. Rational reflection is treated as a delayed reaction to the perpetual forward motion of one's historical existence. "Existence precedes essence" and that is basic freedom. As Sartre has said, "The essence of the human being is in suspense in his freedom."[1]

Thomists often lump themselves irenically with existentialists in order to inspire a common front against various idealisms. Idealisms are essentialist philosophies. All reality is regarded as a process of realizing a rational scheme which is the germinal substance of life, the essence. For idealisms, essence precedes existence. For Thomism and scholasticism, existence precedes essence in the order of knowing because "nothing is in thought which is not first in thing." Even in the order of being, man has his essence only in potentiality. His existence is a dynamic evolution, an actualization of his essence. Basically, however, scholasticism is also an essentialist philosophy. In its view of God essence and existence are equated, and in its view of man existence is predisposed by essence in the same way the oak is predisposed by the acorn. That locates reality always somehow only in the past.

Vitalist and existential philosophies regard this kind of rational, structural predisposition as a denial of freedom for a future and therefore for history. By attributing priority to existence rather than to essence everywhere in reality, they mean to affirm that man is free and that therefore the universe is on the side of history. In so doing the meaning of essence is revised. Essence to the vitalist is not a rational structure in life which existence simply elucidates. Essence is itself the elucidation of the meaning realized

[1] L'être et le néant, Paris, 1948, p. 61.

in the free acts of one's existence. Hereafter, "It is not adequate
to say 'be reasonable' but rather 'be reasonable out of existence.' "[2]

No one has stated the case for scholasticism as an existentialism
more curiously than Etienne Gilson. "The philosophy of St.
Thomas is existential in the fullest sense of the word. . . . As a
philosophy of the act-of-being (i.e., a philosophy which establishes
the existence of God) Thomism is not another existential philosophy, it is the only one."[3] Here a stubborn apologist has
emerged from beneath the scholar's robe. What Thomism means
by existentialism is the mediation of truth through concrete
realities. Modern existentialism means that too. But the "concrete"
for Thomism is defined as reality perceptible to the senses. To
existentialism this can be the most abstract reality, as the empirical
sciences sometimes illustrate. In relation to nature, the self, which
is an historical reality, is most apt to be forgotten, and the historical is the most concrete reality. Thomists may be right in claiming paternity of the term "existentialism," and they are surely right
in claiming Thomism as an existentialism in contrast to essentialist
philosophies which sponsor unmediated intuitions of God. But
they are wrong in regarding the mediation of "nature" as the sign
of a concrete existentialism. The lie to this from the theological
side is in the fact that Gilson in his exposition of Thomist thought
treats "nature" as "creation," whereas in Biblical theology creation
is a category primarily of history. Nature is known as creation
only when persons know who the creator is. This knowledge is
historically mediated. Thomas, aping Aristotle, would say that
nothing is in thought which is not first in sense. Existentialism
would say that nothing is significant in thought which is not first
in history, that is, lived through by a self.

A list of the recent pioneers in the concept of freedom at the

[2] Karl Jaspers, *Vernunft und Existenz*, Groningen, 1935, p. 92.
[3] *The Christian Philosophy of St. Thomas Aquinas*, tr. by L. K. Shook,
Random House, pp. 367-68. I am drawing here upon my review of this book
in *The Christian Century*, February 13, 1957, pp. 199, 200.

base of history would include Kierkegaard, Nietzsche, and Dostoevsky; Marx, Freud, and Dewey; Bergson and (in a limited way) Whitehead; and a growing list of contemporary existentialists—the so-called atheistic Heidegger, Sartre, Camus, and Simone de Beauvoir; the theistic Jaspers; and the very theological existentialists—Jewish Buber, Roman Catholic Marcel, and Orthodox Berdyaev. All these philosophers seem agreed at the two points which place them beyond Plato and Kant, beyond rationalism and moralism.

In the first place, these recent philosophies do not fear, as the Greeks did, that nature will thwart freedom. A seemingly Biblical anthropology animates their thought. The human body is believed to be organic with the total self rather than hostile toward it. Moreover, a kind of biological evolutionism is affirmed which sees in nature a continuous process of agile adaptation more suggestive of freedom than of necessity. What Marcel Proust called "botanical metaphors" abound in their writings.

The real enemy of freedom, it is believed, is not nature but reason. Reason is an excellent instrument for insight into past necessities, but it falters in what John Dewey calls "foresight into possibility" or what Whitehead calls "advance into novelty." "Transcendence of mere clarity and order is necessary for dealing with the unforeseen, for progress, for excitement."[4] When existence precedes essence a kind of history comes into being in which "the past loses its unique precedence"[5] and future possibilities overshadow accomplished facts.

Reason is, moreover, an indispensable agent in the analysis of life, but it is the misfortune of reason that when it analyzes it must "stop and think" and thereby miss the many-splendored moving scene. Cocteau once complained in a letter to Maritain he was so busy writing The Parade he never got to see one. Van Gogh deplored having to kill the butterfly he wished to paint. One can-

4 Alfred North Whitehead, Modes of Thought, Macmillan, 1938, p. 108.
5 Martin Heidegger, Sein und Zeit, Halle, 1927, p. 391.

not sketch life from death. But it is inseparable from the operations of the reason, so these vitalists believe, to take "a snapshot of the mobility of the inner life" (Bergson), to portray the whole of life in abstractions and fragments. "The letter killeth" and the reason deals in letters. How, then, shall reason live with the spirited mobilities of art, of love, of religion—which is to say, of history. "We are free," said Bergson, "when our acts spring from the *whole* personality."[6]

In the second place, these contemporary philosophers are not, as Kant was, enamored of moral responsibility. That is, they have no taste for what Romano-Germanic culture calls responsibility, accountability, and the imputability of moral guilt. Irresponsibility in the newer sense is not a moral or a legal notion, it is an historical notion. Irresponsibility does not denote a fault to be imputed; it is a default of responsibility. One ought not ask, "Was his act conscious and deliberate?" One ought to ask, "Was his act whole?" Wholeness is an attribute neither of consciousness nor of rational deliberation, but of the hidden unity and destiny of the personality which is his history. Irresponsibility, then, is a sickness, and responsibility is its opposite, personal wholeness and health and responsiveness to one's historical vocation.

Actually, the sickness of the personality is often incurred by its very conscious and deliberate effort to conform to the rational and moral. Nietzsche and Freud contribute spectacular evidence of this. Bad conscience, they say, is a disease the personality contracts. It is "a reaction-formation" which follows when its instinct for freedom is "forced back, trodden back, imprisoned within itself and finally only able to find vent and relief in itself." The bad conscience is the sense of oppressiveness in a life whose proper vitality is stifled by codes that have no necessary relation to the emerging needs of the human spirit but which, for the proprieties and emotional loyalties that surround them, compel the spirit to

[6] *Time and Free Will*, Macmillan, 1913, p. 172.

hypocritical submission. "The soul, whose will is cloven in two within itself" says to itself, "I'm sick of myself!"

> The *sick*, then, are the great danger of man, *not* the evil, not the 'beasts of prey.' . . . Oh, how they themselves are ready in their hearts to *exact* penance, how they thirst after being hangmen![7]

Whatever freedom is, then, it is believed there are aspirations associated with man's freedom toward which the reason is unsympathetic. The intellect, as Karl Heim once said, is "an archive director." But man is a history-making, not simply a history-recording, animal. Life and desire and the quest for authenticity, better known to religious tradition as faith or salvation supercede the restrictions of mere correctness.

> You see, gentlemen, reason is an excellent thing, there's no disputing that, but reason is nothing but reason, and satisfies only the rational side of man's nature, while will is a manifestation of the whole life, that is, of the whole human life including reason and all the impulses. . . . Reason only knows what it has succeeded in learning . . . and human nature acts as a whole, with everything that is in it, consciously or unconsciously, and even if it goes wrong, it lives.

So Dostoevsky writes in his *Notes from the Underground*.[8] Ordinarily, one's choices will conform to what commends itself to consciousness as rational. But there is a point at which one may even will to be stupid, "in order," as Dostoevsky says, "not to be bound by an obligation to desire only what is sensible."

This Russian wildness is reminiscent of Tertullian's *credo quia absurdum*. The famous phrase is apochryphal, but Tertullian has said what amounts to the same. "Credibile est, quia ineptum est. . . . Certum est, quia impossibile est."[9] With the context,

---

[7] Nietzsche, "Genealogy of Morals," *The Philosophy of Nietzsche*, Modern Library Edition, pp. 748, 9.
[8] *Short Novels*, Dial, p. 147.
[9] *On the Flesh of Christ*, 5.

the usual translation reads, "The son of God died; it is by all means to be believed, because it is absurd. (*ineptum*) And He was buried, and rose again; the fact is certain (*certum est*) because it is impossible." Everything depends on *certum est*, which does not really mean "certain" at all, but just the opposite. *Certum* in Roman law—and Tertullian was a lawyer in the Roman tradition—means resolution. It pertains not to a certainty, but to the kind of action one must take in the absence of certainty. *Certum* is a rhetorical parallel to *credibile*. Each interprets the other. When one does not know "for certain" and the issue is nevertheless crucial, one must resolve. The faithful man is not the rational man but the resolute man, and resolution takes place in freedom. What is impossible to reason is possible to freedom.

What then shall one say of moral responsibility where one decides to enter into affiliations in the absence of rational certainty and transparency? Descartes and Kant would answer, "immoral—the antithesis of freedom." Tertullian's answer is given in his *Prescription against Heretics*: "There is impunity in erring if there is no delinquency." For Tertullian knew what the sceptics of the Middle Academy at Athens knew. He knew that significant action ought not wait upon rational clarity if in fact the things that matter most cannot be rationally penetrated.

This position is comparable to that taken by the so-called "modern Tertullian," Kierkegaard. Kierkegaard believed that so long as the mode of one's relationship is in the truth, "the individual is in the truth even if he should happen to be thus related to what is not true."

> An objective uncertainty held fast in an appropriation-process of the most passionate inwardness is the truth, the highest attainable for an existing individual. . . . The truth is precisely a venture which chooses an objective uncertainty. . . . The above definition of truth is an equivalent expression for faith. . . . If I am capable of grasping God

objectively, I do not believe, but precisely because I cannot do this I must believe.[10]

Moral responsibility, which presupposes the consciousness of clear and distinct ideas, is utterly appropriate in matters involving the true and the false, the good and the evil, the right and the wrong. How does it fare, however, where one's whole life is involved—his history, his loves and hates, his loyalties and lies, his humility and his pride, his life and his death, his fundamental meaning? When one's existential history is the issue, "there is impunity in erring if there is no delinquency." In the spirited resoluteness of freedom there is a talent which ranges beyond the level of conscious and deliberate choice. "The free act is," as Sartre says, "absurd, beyond all reason."[11] That is to say, existence precedes essence as resolution precedes reflection and love precedes calculation. The human reason is an instrument of our historical existence. But our historical existence is of the stuff of freedom, which is the possibility of deciding whether our on-going life has some supportive meaning.

II. FUTURE POSSIBILITY AS FREEDOM

What is this "freedom" which these recent philosophies have set up against previous philosophical definitions? And how does it relate to what is meant by history?

The radicalism of the view is that freedom is the human existence. One cannot simply say that man is a "something" with the function of freedom. Man is his freedom. Attributes and functions cannot be equated with what man really is. It can be said that man thinks, wills, and feels. But it cannot be said he is thought, will, and feeling. It can be said, however, that man is his freedom. Man is a being who exists by doing. He is not a nature with attributes. He is history. Man is his resolute acts, his freedom.

[10] Concluding Unscientific Postscript, Princeton University Press, 1941, p. 182.
[11] L'être et le néant, p. 559.

As Sartre has said it, "I am my own freedom."[1] Or as Jaspers has said it,

> In the resolve I experience the freedom in which I decide not merely about something but about myself. . . . I myself am the freedom of this choice. Pure choice appears only as a choice between objectivities; but freedom is as the choice of myself.[2]

Or as Kierkegaard has said, when one does not choose, one withers away in consumption.

According to existentialism, however, freedom is nothing. One experiences a "vast and pointless sense of freedom" (Sartre) when contemplating the world about him. As I have previously shown, Pascal knew the sensation when he contemplated the infinity and absurdity of the universe which seventeenth century science had uncovered; the seventeenth century preacher, John Donne, knew it when he announced in the phrase which has now become familiar, " 'Tis all in peeces, all cohaerence gone"; Wordsworth knew it when he referred to this same universe as a nothing in which one is "forlorn" but for some creed. In the words of Pascal,

> When I consider the short duration of my life, swallowed up in the eternity before and after, the little space which I fill, and even can see, engulfed in the infinite immensity of spaces of which I am ignorant, and which know me not, I am frightened, and am astonished at being here rather than there; for there is no reason why here rather than there, why now rather than then.[3]

Sartre described the sensation in his novel, Nausea. When the young man sitting on a park bench contemplates the root of a tree, and it blurs, fades, and otherwise illustrates evanescence, the young man becomes sick. The clue to his sickness is his discovery that existence is radically contingent. That is, there is no reason

---

[1] The Reprieve, p. 362.
[2] Philosophie, Vol. II, Berlin, 1932, p. 182.
[3] Pensées, fragment 205.

for existence, there is nothing *in* existence that explains it. A fundamental difference between the ancient and the modern views of the world is thereby marked. The ancient was alternately annoyed by cosmic necessity and edified by cosmic orderliness. The modern is sickened by cosmic contingency. The more comforting cosmology of antiquity is thus replaced in modern times by an intense life-feeling which Wilhelm Dilthey has characterized as a "feeling incapable of being solved by demonstration," "an insoluble metaphysical void at the bottom of every consciousness."[4] "Inside, nothing, not even a puff of smoke, there is no inside, there is nothing. Myself: nothing. I am free, he said to himself, and his mouth was dry."[5] This void, this nothing is man's freedom. As Jaspers says, "Freedom is where a series is begun out of nothing."[6]

Yet, it is believed that freedom is possibility. The "nothing" of freedom is a "lack" (Sartre), but a "lack" is a possibility. To classical philosophy "possible" meant "noncontradictory." To contemporary existentialism "possible" means a lack to be filled. "Nothing" is a possibility in existence which accounts for the striving, desiring, and seeking by which human life is constantly attempting to fulfill itself. The complement of the sickening sensation of being tied to nothing, of swimming over 70,000 fathoms (Kierkegaard) is the fascinating possibility of going somewhere and being something. Freedom is "a vibrating needle" (Buber), a "viscosity" (Sartre), an urge toward unforeseen possibilities, an indefinable sense of being "for the sake of" something. (Heidegger)

Existential nihilism does not claim that man is "nothing at all." It simply says that he is not yet what he can be. A nihilist in existential parlance can be defined as Nietzsche did it in *The Will to Power*. (Ch. xvi) He "judges of the world as it is that it ought

[4] From "Einleitung in die Geisteswissenschaften," *Gesammelte Schriften*, Vol. I, Leipzig and Berlin, 1914, p. 364.
[5] Sartre, *The Reprieve*, p. 362.
[6] *Philosophie*, Vol. II, p. 188.

not be and of the world as it ought to be that it does not exist."
Man's nothingness is, as Emmanuel Mounier once said, "a state
of something not coinciding with itself." Calvin was right, therefore, in the *Institutes* to distinguish between *nullus* and *nihil* and
apply only *nihil* to man. (I, i, 3) (This distinction is conserved in
Greek as οὐκ ὄν and μή ὄν.)

Man exists in so far as he is the being who stretches out beyond
himself. As Flaubert has said, "If the feeling of human insuffi-
ciency, of the nothingness of life, were to perish . . . we should be
more stupid than the birds." Animals do not exist. They lack,
but have no sense of lack. They are "in themselves" but not "for
themselves." Nor does God exist. He lacks nothing. He is both
"in and for himself." Man is the being who suffers the encounter
with nothingness, which is the gap between his sheer facticity and
his project, his past and his future. The prefix "ex-" specifies this
movement toward the future which is the centrifugal tendency in
the being of an existing man.

Almost anyone would say the same of man. He is a being who
is not what he can be. But philosophy has rarely defined man as
that interval itself. Man *is* not a substance which is constantly
undergoing tension and revision. Man *is* the tension. He *is* the
process of revision. He is not the beginning and he is not the
end. He is the tight-rope dance between. He is not the abyss
beneath, either. He is the *inter-esse*, a being between what
was and what will come. The past which is what he was is no
more the reality he is than the future which is what he will become. He is the reality which is the relation between these possibilities.

This view is known to philosophy as actualism. Man is his act.
The philosopher Fichte espoused it radically. In *The Science of
Knowledge*, "the Ego is not something which has powers. It is
simply acting. It is what it acts, and when it does not act it is
not at all." Sartre has illustrated this actualism in claiming that
there is no ego while one is driving a car or reading a book, pre-

sumably because there is no sense of relation, or decision, or being present to oneself, although anyone who has driven in Paris or read a novel by Sartre must know he chooses some misleading analogies.

From as early as childhood it is possible to exist, to sense yourself weighing upon yourself in the act of transition to the future. Stop an anxious child and ask him what the trouble is. He will almost always answer, "Nothing!" He is only in a face-to-face struggle for his own arrival as a person. Interrogate a friend in a moment when his eyes seem vacuous. "What's on your mind?" He may reply, "Oh, nothing!" But he may also be stretched midway between the poles of his existence. He *is* the field of force between. Man is, as Heidegger has said, a being thrown into the world. His life is a continuous process of throwing himself back. Where, to whom, and why? These questions haunt the process and make him feel his life more poignantly. But the act of receiving and throwing back his life is his existence. "Who can possess what he himself must hold, what he from time to time only catches and throws again as a child a ball!" (Rilke)

To call man "nothing," then, does not down-grade him. It simply locates him in terms of his responsibility in the realm of beings. Man is when he relates, when he acts, when he decides. And if he does not act at all? Then he evaporates. This is the terrible burden of freedom that comes with being a man. Sartre's novels are full of it. Man is to Sartre a viscous being whose shape changes with his every act, a puff of smoke which comes and goes to the extent that one keeps materializing himself in action. "What are you thinking about?" "Nothing!" But his mouth will be dry with the panic which comes from knowing he will be what he decides.

But has not God created us? Do we not therefore substantially exist regardless of our acts? To talk that way is to belittle both the creator and the creature. Existentialism helps us overcome that substantialistic, scholastic prejudice by leading us in the direction of a Biblical view of man. For creation is not the simple process of constructing what Plato called a "featherless bi-ped." Creation is God's invocation to a life of responsibility. Creation is not a cosmological, but a historical concept. Man as creature is the existing man. He is the man who is stretching himself between the facticity of his simply being there and the project which is his response to God's invocation. Judged by that standard, an existentialist himself may be no more than what Dostoevsky called "an ungrateful bi-ped," for he does not adopt God's call as his project. But he will be more than most men are who define man only by his relation to the animal. Man, unlike the animal, exists. That is, he constantly moves beyond himself in self-transcending acts, beyond the past, which is what he must be, to the future, which is what he may be. As Nietzsche has Zarathustra say in the lines which inspired Morton Wishengrad's play "The Rope Dancers," "Man is a cord above an abyss. A perilous arriving, a perilous traveling, a perilous looking backward, a perilous trembling and standing still. What is great in man is that he is a bridge, and no goal." One's faith may save one's history from the abyss beneath by turning the existential rope dance into an act of *sursum corda*.

Freedom is a burden, and man feels "condemned forever to be free" (Sartre) because as freedom, "the human existence is the locus of the possible failure of being."[7] That is, man can choose himself as nothing or in relation to some possibility beyond himself. He can reach beyond himself to some relationship that may confer a meaning which is not intrinsic to his existence. "Freedom is not an indifferent will but the possibility of being free for something."[8]

The risk of freedom, however, is that it is possible for one to relate himself to what itself participates in the nothingness, contingency, and absurdity of existence. Religion calls this idolatry,

[7] Paul Tillich, *Religiöse Verwirklichung*, Berlin, 1930, pp. 36 and 39.
[8] Heidegger, *Sein und Zeit*, p. 144.

and philosophy calls it nihilism. Neither atheistic nor theistic existentialism knows of an ultimately secure relationship, though both know that man is haunted by a desire for a fulfillment he is never able to achieve. Atheistic existentialism sometimes leaves the possibility open and remains wistful (as in Heidegger), sometimes rejects the possibility and becomes Stoical (as in Sartre). That one must make this choice is the burden of one's freedom. That he must do it without the certain knowledge of any actual basis for his choice intensifies the burden.

Such a choice is equally burdensome to the theistic existentialist, for when he chooses a relation to the transcendent, non-contingent reality he calls God, he chooses what he does not know but simply believes or hopes. This is his freedom. As Jaspers says, "I am free because I do not know," or as Marcel says, freedom is to "decide . . . without any appeal."

Freedom is, then, a terrifying burden, the burden of a desperately serious lack, a burden so terrifying it has become the source of an endemic human sickness recognized in life today as anxiety. As freedom, man may choose either to be what he is or to affiliate with sources of authenticity beyond himself. This freedom is not simply the ability to choose but the inability not to choose. (Simone de Beauvoir) The choice is between contingency and loyalty, between a dying independence and a living dependence, between hopelessness without obligation and hope with obligation. One desires existence on his own terms but fears if he "bows down to nothing he cannot bear the burden of himself." (Dostoevsky) One fears to pledge himself yet desires the authenticity which right relationship confers. The collision of fear and desire is the friction in freedom which we know to be anxiety, the rubbing together of nothingness and possibility. Anxiety is a condition that paralyzes action and obscures whatever transparency man has at the very moment he needs it the most, the moment in which his destiny, his very being, his life and death are being determined.

The predicament of man is a predicament born of freedom, a sickness Balzac called "a tetanus of the soul."

The widespread practice of deploring any reference to sickness as a symptom of pessimism is on the wane. Circles that deal in the therapy of the mind know that nothing so obstructs the therapeutic process as a fictitious sense of health. "Anxiety is the ground of hope," said Jaspers, who was himself a psychiatrist before he was an existential philosopher. It is the human ground of hope, to be sure, and of a hope that is by no means decisive. For one can learn "to love despair" (Lord Byron), because "in despair there are the most intense enjoyments." (Dostoevsky)

Nevertheless, it remains true that the possibility of this sickness is, as Kierkegaard said, "man's advantage over the beast." It is the sign of man's historicity, his having a destiny. "How regard this voyage as without destination," Melville wrote in *The White Jacket*, "when upon our first embarkation as infants the violent rollings makes every soul of us sea-sick." One has to be a little sick before one "feels oneself existing," said Maine de Biran. But Nietzsche pointed out how the sickness can be like a pregnancy which one can get over and have something to show for besides. The sickness of anxiety is a sickness not in our nature but in our history which reminds us we have a destiny. It is a nostalgia to remind us that our tour through the world has God at its beginning and its end.

III. FREEDOM THE SOURCE OF REASON

Existential history is the sickness of freedom in history. In it one experiences the possibility of a future which is not simply an inference from his past. In a pre-Christian or secularized way, therefore, existential history embraces what theology understands by the image of God in man and by original sin.

The *image of God* has generally been believed to be some fundamental likeness man has to God, some resemblance such as one would expect to see between a father and his son. This resemblance has usually been identified with man's rationality. Theology, however, has been embarrassed to find the sense of the likeness between God and man inspiring self-satisfaction rather than filial loyalty and responsibility. Moreover, there has been a restlessness in theology respecting the way in which affirmations of man's likeness to God disregard the irreversible structure in a relation that exists between Creator and creature. In protest against this genetic definition of "likeness" the theologian has urged that the image of God is to be found in one man only, in Jesus Christ, who is appropriately called God's only son.

What, then, of the image of God in other men than Jesus? The image of God in man is the human possibility for man's relationship to God. That possibility is freedom, and freedom is responsibility, or the ability *to be* at God's disposal. Not freedom, then, as Aristotle defined it when he said "man is free . . . who exists for his own sake and not for another's." (*Metaphysics* I, 2) Not even freedom as, for instance, Philo defined it when he regarded freedom in man as the quality that most resembles God, the power of interrupting the laws of nature. It is rather a freedom which is not at all like God's because it is a freedom for dependence, a burdensome and restless freedom, a freedom which fulfills itself only in dependence upon God. "Existence precedes essence." It is simply not true that a person first perceives God, and then, as it were, puts himself in relation to him. The effort to establish relation comes first. God made us out of the nothing of freedom and our souls are restless until they choose themselves in him.

The *doctrine of original sin* has been retained in contemporary theology as an interpretative clue to the gravity of human life. It is difficult, however, in doctrines of original sin for theologians to satisfy the demands both of morality and of historicity. Generally whatever the original sin is, no one is expected to assume responsibility for it, inasmuch as it was precipitated without one's own conscious, deliberate choice. It is a Kantian requirement that an accountable act be voluntary and conscious, but there are two difficulties with this moral requirement.

The first problem is that our destiny-determining acts are so profound we cannot subject them to analysis. We can only pre-suppose them. As Balzac has said of our wounds, "we cannot examine them, they hurt too much." Or, as Sartre has said, "Con-scious deliberation is always faked. . . . When I deliberate the die is already cast. . . . The decision has already been taken."[1] Original sin is the spiritual tension at the root of our lives that vitiates all our acts—rational and voluntary—without either our knowledge or our choice. This is what Luther meant by his doctrine of the bondage of the will, and probably Augustine, too. It does not mean we are not free. Man *is* freedom. It does mean our free-dom is a sick and anxious freedom which knows it must embark but does not know its destination. Ever since the Apostle Paul, it has been known in the Christian tradition that the problem of freedom is not the problem of choice (*velle*) but of ability (*posse*), not legislation but execution, not ends but energy.

The second problem in a strictly moral definition of original sin is that guilt is denied to original sin because such an original act was not "freely," that is, consciously and deliberately com-mitted. Hence, responsibility for the declivity in one's life also seems abrogated. What if guilt, however, were not something legally imputable, as if sin were a crime, an aberration traceable to a specific act of offense? What if guilt were a condition of being, a condition of deeper, personal irresponsibility, a default of voca-tion, a gap in our history? Formally, guilt is the disproportion between what one is and what one ought to be. Actually, what if guilt were not simply the failure to achieve recognized moral ends but the condition of being at odds with one's spiritual destiny? What if guilt were not a result, but a *condition* of doing wrong. That is, not a doing wrong at all, but a being wrong? Not an isolated act in our freedom, but the whole direction in our free-

[1] *L'être et le néant*, p. 527.

dom—our very history? "Being guilty," says Martin Heidegger, "does not result originally from a fault; faults originally become possible on the basis of an original guilt."[2] "Being guilty" is a sickness of freedom; not a fault to be condemned, but a sickness to be cured. There is responsibility in sickness, but it is not legal or moral responsibility. One is not blamed for being sick, but he is expected to *assume* responsibility for it as the first step to a cure. That is why for a long time now the story of Adam has dawned on men with the abruptness and lucidity that comes when one "suddenly remembers where he left his glasses." (T. S. Eliot)

These acts of responsibility and default registered as existential history are often dismissed as irrational. By that is meant they usually proceed upon some other basis than the objective caution tutored by the empirical and logical sciences. They are called "leaps" because they respond to hidden and interior urgencies undetected by the instruments which transcribe objective matters. They are called irrational because they rest upon decisions or commitments which, arrogating to themselves the executive power, reduce the rational function to the level of the legislative only.

By these standards, however, these acts should not be called irrational but sur-rational. Existential history does not proceed in violation or disregard of the legislative reason. It only negotiates with life at a profounder than legislative level. As Samuel Taylor Coleridge says, you can only claim these acts are higher than the reason in the same way you claim the roots of a tree are higher than its branches. Or, in Jaspers' now familiar slogan, do not say "Be reasonable!" Say, "Be reasonable out of existence." "Existence precedes essence," as the existential formula goes, which means "My existential experience is anterior to my knowledge of it." (Berdyaev) Our rational thought is what John Dewey called "the intellectual voucher" of transactions deeply rooted in our existence. Vouchers are an indispensable index to what is taking place. But vouchers are not legal tender. Thoughts become abstract and im-

² *Sein und Zeit*, p. 280.

potent in the same way languages become dead when, by virtue of their detachment from our history, they lose the capacity to translate our ongoing life meaningfully.

Existential acts are the acts in which we choose who we will be and by that choice become who we are. These acts are leaps not because they are blind, but because they are the way we have of spanning the chasm between our past and our future, our facticity and our project, our sheer brute being and our ultimate vocation. The existentialist who inspires leaps in life is not pandering to mankind's petulance or to the immaturity which values kicks more highly than contemplation. He is alerting man to his very life. Man is a deciding being whose very reality is at stake in his commitments and for whom there is only one thing worse than choosing what is wrong. That is not choosing at all.

Bertrand Russell is accepted by many as a safe guide when he claims that "Morally, a philosopher who uses his profound competence for anything except a disinterested search for truth is guilty of a kind of treachery." When it is known, however, that the philosopher as a man is an *inter-esse*, a being between, who is his history and whose history is in suspense in his commitments, it appears as the deeper betrayal of existence to make one's search disinterested.

Sartre may be the more reliable guide just because he chooses his analogies from the art of love and not from the empirical sciences. As he says in his novel, *Nausea*, "You know, it's quite a job starting to love somebody. You have to have energy, generosity, blindness. There is even, in the very beginning, when you have to jump across a precipice: if you think about it you don't do it." Or, as St. John of the Cross has put it, "In love you do not ask what reason wants to know: it is against the rules."

The risk and the subjectivism in this line are a scandal to a philosophical culture whose dominant academic philosophies are scientific. W. H. Auden has a poem called "Leap before you Look," but I remember hearing him comment on Kierkegaard to the effect that it was the devil who first suggested Jesus should leap from the pinnacle. Existentialism ought not be regarded as a suggestion of the devil, considering today's philosophical climate. The existential insistence that life cannot be adequately negotiated on the basis of a single mode of spiritual activity is imperative where the sole mode being recommended is the one instructed by the empirical sciences.

There is the "pure reason" of the technological method where one thinks on things and counts them. But in that method a gap always remains between our ideas and ourselves. It ought to. That is the genius of the objective sciences. They cannot and should not proceed without an object. But there is also the "historical reason." The historical reason is the process of reasoning from freedom. It does not hold its ideas in separation from its life. It counts on them.

In a discussion on a college campus recently a co-ed blandly informed me she believed in nothing. I raised what seemed to me to be the next step in the dialogue and gently asked, "What are you now living by?" I think I saw the girl evaporate before my very eyes. It is to her credit. Some would have remained suspended in air, pursuing the illusion that man, like some southern mosses, can survive without a root which commits his life. Alain Robbe-Grillet has called this attitude "voyeurism" and has chosen as his heroes men "affected with undue visual curiosity." Sartre has called the attitude the Actaeon complex. Actaeon on a hunt one day cleared away the branches to have a better view of Diana at her bath. The man who approaches all life with only one method, the objective rationality of the scientist, is like "the hunter who surprises a white nudity and who violates by looking at it." At the historical level the observer attitude is the crudest obscenity. It can be ended only by an act of decisiveness in which the gap between observer and observed is overcome and marriage makes them one.

CHAPTER

4

HISTORY, THE MIND'S ITINERARY

EXISTENTIAL history can be said to be a form of mysticism. As has been seen in the foregoing accounts, when the existing man is pressed by the question of the ultimate possibility of things, he experiences himself quite vividly. The experience of oneself takes on the aspect of a demand. The question of the meaning of existence requires a man to resolve himself, even in the absence of final evidence that such a possibility is supportable. What the reason cannot dictate to the man, the man in his freedom must supply to the reason. A reason which admits the priority of freedom in its judgments is an historical reason, and its itinerary closely resembles the passionate, committed way of life one associates with mysticism.

Like mysticism, existential history is a way of life and a view of life. As a way of life it is something anybody can engage in without analyzing it. It is a kind of style of existence. As a view of life it is a philosophy of existence, a world-view quite consciously stylized after the modes of thought developed among philosophers since the beginning. The way of existential history is through the tragic sense of life, a dryness and thirst which keeps man continually *en route*. Existentialism strikingly resembles mysticism in this respect. But mysticism moves into the bubbling fountain of the being of God. Existentialism is always *en route*, always historical, always between nature and God, with no clue to the existence of an oasis but the parched sand and the tantalizing mirage. Those who underestimate this difference between existentialism and mysticism expect either too much from a philosophy or too little from a faith. When a mystic gives conscious expression to his way of life, he has praise only for God. For the mystic way is at last consummated not by man's ascent but by God's descent, so that mysticism is a way of life and a theology. But existentialism is a way of life and a philosophy, and a philosopher has only the clues that are present in the world. The philosopher as philosopher has no access to eternity. He is a creature of time. Not only is he in time; time is in him. As one who takes time to tell the meaning of time, he can repeat only what time tells him. Somerset Maugham has not overstated the case, then, in A Writer's Notebook:

> The philosopher is like a mountaineer who has with difficulty climbed a mountain for the sake of the sunrise, and arriving at the top finds only fog; whereupon he wanders down again. He must be an honest man if he doesn't tell you that the spectacle was stupendous.

It is possible, however, to exaggerate the difference between mysticism and existentialism, between the consummation of a revealed faith and the consuming passion of a point of view in world history. Existential history is a tragic sense in the world's history because it sees history without God and hence with nowhere to go. Mystics conserve that same tragic sense, up to the point where they experience relief in God's incarnation into human experience as the end of history. The parallel between the two in respect of their tragic sense is highly instructive. It contributes to an understanding of the existential dimension of history and to an appreciation of the theological intimations in existential history.[1]

---

[1] Some aspects of this correlation are suggested by Gordon E. Michalson, *Baron Friedrich von Hügel and Søren Kierkegaard*, unpublished doctoral dissertation, Drew University, Madison, N. J., 1946.

I. PENULTIMATE MYSTICISM

Existentialism as a point of view has become a kind of secularized mysticism. By this I do not mean that it has plagiarized into a philosophy the insights of mystical theology, insights unavailable to its own methods—although there is some basis for this charge. A family tree of contemporary existentialism would show a fairly direct line from the existential *dramatis personae* to the mystics of the past. Karl Jaspers and Nicolas Berdyaev, for instance, are inconceivable without Jacob Boehme and Boehme's philosophical successor, Schelling. Martin Buber roots in the Jewish mysticism known as Chasidism. Gabriel Marcel is linked to Bergson and F. H. Bradley, both of whom avow mystical dependencies. Miguel de Unamuno and Ortega y Gasset are philosophical translations of the Spanish mystics, Theresa of Avila and John of the Cross. Martin Heidegger and Jean-Paul Sartre develop the phenomenology of Husserl, with the rise of which, as Paul Tillich says, "a mystical element has entered into modern philosophy." Whether the Austrian poet Rilke is an existential philosopher depends on whether one is willing to concede with Hölderlin that philosophy is simply "a hospital for wrecked poets." Nevertheless, Rilke, like the German poet Hölderlin himself, goes behind the western Christian development to the pagan sources of western mysticism in Neo-Platonism and Orphism. Hence, he holds a muscular sort of pre-Christian existentialism characteristic of so much of the thought of so pivotal a mystical theologian as Augustine, who drew on these same sources.

By calling existential philosophy a secularized mysticism I mean rather that it is a kind of laicized mysticism. It is an approach to life that has out-flanked conventional, institutionalized, and ordained religious and metaphysical quests. In the process it has tasted the depths of the human predicament as few religious or non-religious thinkers have. In that form it closely resembles patterns developed at the penultimate stage of mysticism, at the

stage, that is, of the thirst for God. If existentialists were able
without reference to established faiths and theistic philosophies
to introduce into culture today only the presentiment of a meaningful reality transcending human experience, it would not be the
first time in the history of western piety that spiritual wistfulness
has broken into life through a spiritually irregular medium.

There are, to be sure, warnings in contemporary theology about
both mysticism and existentialism. One ought not forget Emil
Brunner's *Die Mystik und das Wort*, an exaggerated but devastat-
ing criticism of Schleiermacher's philosophical mysticism and of
Evelyn Underhill's psychological mysticism. The way to God, he
made quite clear, is not through interior human experience but
through God's own self-revelation and his concrete, historical word
in Jesus Christ. Even Karl Barth, who in his *Römerbrief* stage was
called "the most mystical of all the anti-mystics," should be heeded.
He warned that mysticism is not a way to God, not even a *via
negativa*, but only a *Holzweg*, a path in the woods which leads
nowhere.

To link existentialism with mysticism, then, would be to call
down upon existentialism radical disapproval from these and other
fathers of our contemporary faith. Indeed, this is currently happening in both Protestantism and Catholicism. In his encyclical,
Humani generis, Pope Pius XII alerted Roman Catholicism to the
twin tendencies of existentialism and mysticism cropping up in
the Roman Church under the tutelage of Biblical and patristic
scholars such as Jean Danièlou, Henri de Lubac, and the Austrian
theologian Karl Rahner. The implication is that one cannot
profitably go behind the fully developed theology and practice of
the Latin Church to its early Greek and apostolic sources, nor
beyond it to some non-scholastic philosophy like existentialism.
And in Protestant circles the authority of the late Dietrich Bonhoeffer,[2] martyr under Hitler to the cause of the confessing church

---

[2] See the forthcoming volume by John D. Godsey, *The Theology of Dietrich
Bonhoeffer*, Westminster.

in Germany, is being vigorously directed against what he called "religious" tendencies in Protestant apologetics, oriented as they are to existentialism. The sense of the need for God, which Bonhoeffer (and Kutter and Barth before him) claimed is sheer religiousness, ought not be held up as the prerequisite for a meaningful encounter with God. John of the Cross was wrong to insist that "the soul must first be placed in emptiness and poverty of spirit, being purged of all support" before it can enjoy the grace of deliverance.

Therefore, I find myself in almost complete agreement with these criticisms of the way in which existentialism is used in theology, except, of course, the parochially protective criticism of the papal encyclical. Official Catholicism is wrong to resist existentialism as an obstetric force upon the body of the faith. A faith learns something about itself whenever it adopts new dialogical partners. But Barth, Brunner, and Bonhoeffer are right to resist the purely anthropological insinuations in mysticism and existentialism, for theology is not to be identified with anthropology.

Is the danger of anthropologizing theology through alliances with existentialism a real one, however? Is not existentialism a mysticism rather than a humanism, and then only a mysticism in the penultimate sense that it is always striving but never arriving? And is that not precisely what the existentialists mean by calling existentialism a humanism. Sartre's book *L'Existentialisme est un humanisme* was published in English simply as *Existentialism*. But if one reads that tiny, lecture-length volume, he will rapidly make a simple discovery. He will find that there is even in this most blatant and impious form of existentialism no such claim to the self-sufficiency of man as one popularly expects in a "humanism." For want of a God and of a permanent human nature man must go it alone, but he will do so not without a sickening sense of the absurdity of it all. Existentialism is a humanism because its fundamental understanding is a transcription of what appears on the consciousness of man when he identifies himself with the route he is taking through the world.

Existentialism *is* a humanism if one means by humanism what Heidegger defines it to mean in his untranslated letter, *Über den "Humanismus."* In this letter he says, "humanism" means that "the nature of Man is essential for the truth of being." Not that man *is* the truth about being, but that man's quest for the truth begins where a man is, inside his own skin, up against the conditions of life which describe his perimeter, that is, in history. Not that man is the last word about the meaning of life, but that he is the most accessible and the most revealing clue to the meaning and that such meaning is most apt to come to him as a man *en route.* It is instructive to discover that the seventeenth-century mystic Weigel wrote a book entitled *Gnothe Seauton,* and that Gilson's book on Bernard of Clairvaux is inscribed by that same mandate from the oracle at Delphi, "Know thyself!" Man is as Hugh of St. Victor said, "another Cain, 'a wanderer and fugitive upon the earth.' In his wanderings he seeks here, now there, for consolation; a fugitive, he seeks to avoid affliction. He is always on the move." (*De Sacramentis* 1, 9, 3) It is significant that the central character in Sartre's series of novels, *Ways to Freedom,* is called Mathieu de la Rue. It is fully as significant as that Camus has called his wandering, wistful "hero" Jean Baptiste.

Existentialism like mysticism is a beginning from within. It is an articulation of self-consciousness *in via* as one's life bruises itself upon the conditions of the world and raises the question about the ultimate significance of it all. It is an engagement with life so thoroughgoing that in the process either one is left exhausted and unsatisfied, or he is met by a source of authenticity from beyond himself. Existentialism like mysticism will settle for no foreshortened perspective or surrogate salvation. Existentialism is, as mysticism, a discipline of thirst. It will drink with satisfaction from no sources that are not deep enough to be pure. The fourteenth century Dominican Henry Suso is a good example of this discipline.

In his *Autobiography* he recounts how, though his residence was bounded by Lake Constance and the river Rhine, he nonetheless abstained from drinking. He had heard his Lord say that although he was Lord of every stream, yet on earth he tasted only vinegar and gall. "If you would be my disciple, therefore, hold fast in your abstention, with patience." Existentialism, in a secular way, is just such a discipline. In a history apparently deficient in meaning, it is a patient waiting for an advent of the very springs of meaning.

To see how this is so, one needs to examine more in detail and a bit more technically what Marcel calls the "histology" of existentialism. One must ask, "What is the tissue of man?" And when one does, he may see how such strident atheists as Sartre and Camus come close to reverent agnostics like Heidegger, Rilke and Hölderlin. It may even be seen from an answer to this question how this group of philosophers maintains an existential authenticity not present in theistic existentialists like Jaspers, Buber, Berdyaev, and Marcel. I am inclined to believe that these latter, more pious existentialists overstep the penultimate limit of their "mysticism" and break the discipline of thirst too soon.

Man is that very specialized form of life denoted by the word from which "existentialism" gets its name. Man is an existence. "Existence," as Kierkegaard has said in his *Concluding Unscientific Postscript*, "separates thought and being, holding them apart in succession." Quite simply, this means that a man cannot "know" about "being" except as he "lives" it. Only after bumping into being with his life can man read off an authentic result in thought.

But man alone is the specialized form of life, the sensitive tissue that can communicate the meaning of being in this way. This is not man's privilege. It is his vocation as a man. It is, in a sense, his terrifying vocation, for the very status of being is at stake in him. Man is, as Tillich has said in his early *Religiöse Verwirklichung*, the locus of the possible failure of being. Man has been entrusted with the care (*Sorge*) of being, to say it as Heidegger does in *Sein und Zeit*. Man is not the Lord but the shepherd of being. Being is his parish and he is the curate. (*Sorge = cura*)

That is why no existentialist is satisfied to define man in relation to some other form of life, least of all the animal. To say he is "a rational animal" is little improvement over saying he is a "featherless bi-ped." They laughed when Diogenes plucked a chicken and, holding it before the crowd, cried, "Plato's man!" The point about man is not that he go beyond the animal but that he go beyond himself in the direction of true being. Max Scheler suggests in *Die Stellung des Menschen im Kosmos* that the difference between Thomas Edison as inventor of the incandescent bulb and the chimpanzee is only a quantitative difference. But the difference between man as the curate of being, who throws himself into life with seriousness and thus elucidates or exegetes the hidden meaning at the base of life—the difference between man as existence and the man who is simply there is qualitative. Tell me why you do what you do, challenged Ortega y Gasset, addressing a monkey in a Spanish zoo, and I will tell you who you are! And it is this question and its answers that divide men from men. This responsibility to ask and answer the question about meaning makes man central in existentialism. He is the sensitive membrane separating being and the meaning of being. He is only fulfilling his vocation as a man when, from his contact with being wherever he engages it, he is reporting its significance.

While the proper study of being is man, the results are not always pretty. "Deep, deep, and still deeper we must go," Melville writes in his *Pierre*, "if we would find out the heart of a man; descending into which is as descending [or, ascending, depending on how you spatialize the abyss] a spiral stair in a shaft, without any end, where that endlessness is only concealed by the spiralness of the stair and the blackness of the shaft." For as an existence, he is a being that is constantly going beyond himself. *Ex-sistere:* to stand beyond. Man is this ec-static being who is constantly rising beyond himself in the direction of the realization of being.

Man is the constant movement between "I am not" and "I will be." (Faulkner) He is always, as Sartre says, both posture and project, both reality and possibility, both in himself and for himself. Thrown into the world of time and space as a marble in mud he interrogates himself for who he is. Nothing in his location explains him. Yet his whole being is caught up in the centrifugal force of nostalgia. From his position he is continually projecting a way beyond his position.

This is his power as existence; but this is his tragedy, too. For there is only one being completely coterminous with his project, and this is, by definition, God. Only God is the fulness of being, and man is the futile effort to become God; the self is transcended by a totality it is never able to be. (Sartre) Man is caught in the plight of Sisyphus. He must always be striving, but he will never achieve. He must learn to live and to die, being a man, refusing to be God, and remaining patient with this limitation. (Camus) He is never *sum*, the "I am." He is always *sursum*, ascending beyond himself. (Marcel) "Man reaches beyond himself" (Heidegger) "in the direction of God." (Calvin)

To refuse to project oneself beyond oneself, hence never to suffer the gap of unfulfillment, is one form of default in the vocation of existence. "That which would remain what it is renounces existence." (Rilke) The other default is to identify oneself pantheistically with the Being who is fulfilled. The shepherd of being must not decline to move for fear of unanticipated hazards; nor may he pose as Lord. Either to resign oneself to being-where-one-is or to pretend to a complete fulfillment in life is a sin against the role of man. One who is not ex-isting is either dead or he is God. Death or deity—either is unbecoming to a man, and this fraudulence shows. It shows as in Camus' novel *The Stranger*, where a chaplain with a dead soul attempts to offer consolation to a condemned man who is himself existing; or as in Hölderlin's poem, *Empedocles:*

Away! I cannot bear the sight of him
Who follows sacred callings like a trade;
His face is false and cold and dead, . . .

II. THE DISCIPLINE OF THIRST

A man who seriously assumes his existence, which is his vocation as the shepherd of being, is ironically rewarded with spiritual anguish. The heart of the existing man will be restless, and he will not know why. He will only know that he must not settle for a rest which is short of his true destination. And he will not know his true destination. He will only know that his very life depends on knowing it. He will be thirsty, but that suffering will be the sign of his ordination in the secular apostolate of all shepherds of being. Restlessness will be the sign of the authenticity of his vocation, and he will discipline his thirst with this restlessness lest he drink too soon and thus from inauthentic springs. The suffering of restlessness is the sign of the penultimate character of the mysticism of an existentialist. The mark of the existing man is his unslaked thirst. His soul is made for God. As an existing man he does not know that. He only knows the thirst of a man without God and that he must not satisfy that thirst inauthentically. Hence, his restlessness is to him an inexplicable wretchedness of a life constantly *in via*.

A man is born with this yearning to travel. He is as the peasant in Holberg's comedy, transferred while drunk to the bed of the Danish prince. When man comes to himself in this world, he has the consciousness that he is not at home here. He suffers a sharp pain of nostalgia for his true home. As the mystic Weigel said, the world is an inn. We seem only guests. Nothing is our own. But man is so hedged about by the conditions of life in the world, and his being thrown into the world is an experience of such gravity, that he has only the faintest and most tenuous clues to who he really is. Or he is as the dreamer in an account by Sartre in *L'être et Néant*. He awakens in his place in the world holding to the world as a dreaming man upon awaking finds himself grasping tightly to the sides of his bed. Man's whole life becomes the question as to why he clings to the world. He does not "recall the nightmare that induced his gesture."

Martin Heidegger has fully developed this theme in *Sein und Zeit*. Man is a *Geworfenheit*. There is "a thrownness" about his life. He is impacted in the world by the gravity of his being put here. But he retains in his being the converse of this centripetal force, the centrifugal urge to return to his beginnings. And Gabriel Marcel's recent contribution to the literature of existentialism is exclusively on this theme. It is called *L'Homme problématique*. The chief problem of man, "l'inquietude humaine," is surveyed through western literature from Augustine to the present. It is most obvious to Marcel that a man will not find his rest until he finds it in God. But then Marcel as a faithful Christian has access to an understanding that is not derivable simply from man's homesickness. The grace of God the Creator is a truth not deducible from the gravity of the human situation. That is why I say existentialism, stopping short of this ultimate truth as it does, is only penultimately a mysticisim. It is a candid and disciplined transcript of how dry it is to live in the world without knowing that it is God who has put you here.

Now, if you were to read the plays and novels of Sartre, you might not immediately sense this dryness. You would find obscenity and bestiality in their most vulgar and depressing forms and in their most refined and exotic forms. You would find little in his entire literature that could not be reduced to the compass of his one short play, *No Exit*. But *No Exit* is the modern man's *Divine Comedy*, except that it is no longer comedy, for the story ends where it begins, in hell. Not only is there no sense of a destination in some Paradise. There is no sense of a pilgrimage even through some purgatory. The hell of life is unrelieved. There are, of course, brief episodes of delight, a multiplicity of ingenious ways to evade the irreducible restlessness of life. Yet these diversions only resemble the contentment of the sick "who change their positions in bed and are happy." (Marcel) Life is hell, and in a very small room. You cannot move very far before you come up against its confining limits.

However, as Karl Jaspers says, "experiencing limit situations and existing are the same." He then goes on to analyze those boundaries which thwart all efforts to make peace with the world. There is the struggle for love, and the struggle for power; the sense of guilt, and the confrontation with death. Every movement in the direction of self-fulfillment in this world runs against these questions. Am I accepted by others? Does my life have worth? Am I free from the condemnation of guilt? Do I die forever? These questions help man clarify the more basic question as to who he is. He is the being who is the question about the significance of being. The answer to this question is not readily available. The question itself is nonetheless irrepressible. The movement from the question to the answer is what the medieval mystic, Bonaventura, called "the mind's true itinerary." The existentialist knows what the mystic knows, namely, that he must keep traveling. To live without an answer is like living over a void, a terrifying abyss. Civilization may be, as Allen Tate once said, "the agreement, slowly arrived at, to let the abyss alone." Existentialists, like the mystics, are in this sense enemies of civilization. They are "alone in the midst of these happy, reasonable voices." (Sartre) The existentialists' destiny is not to evade the abyss but to identify it. Their vocation is not to get rid of the discomfort of staring into the void of the world's meaninglessness, but rather to understand the meaning of it. Unable to possess this meaning for themselves, they grow sick from the absurdity of the world.

But this sickness is what Kierkegaard approvingly quotes Hamann as calling a "holy hypochondria." John of the Cross called it "the mystical fever." Just because it finds no satisfaction in history, it keeps alive the wistfulness for something at the limit of history.

Mysticism has an answer for this wistfulness. In the words of Bonaventura,

> Since a man must lie in the spot where he falls, unless someone sets to work and helps him to rise, our souls could not be perfectly raised . . . had not Truth, taking on human form in Christ, become a stair for it, repairing the former stair, which in Adam had been broken down. Hence, however far a man may be illuminated by the light of nature and acquired science, he cannot enter into himself, to enjoy himself in the Lord, save through the Mediation of Christ, who says, 'I am the door.'[1]

But this is the *ultimate* mysticism, the cure of the disease of worldliness, the authentic fountain of life for the thirst of the human existence. The itinerary of existential history extends no further than wistfulness. Being a penultimate mysticism, it simply says,

> A man must lie in the spot where he falls, unless someone sets to work and helps him to rise.

In the novels of Sartre there is a recurrent juxtaposition of two characteristically mystical expressions, "nothingness" and "thirst." "Inside, nothing, not even a puff of smoke, there is no *inside*, there is nothing. Myself: nothing. I am free, he said to himself, and his mouth was dry." Or, again, from the same novel, *The Reprieve*, "That's what existence means: draining one's own self dry with the sense of thirst."

Thirst is the panic symptom that comes from looking into the abyss, which is one's own nothingness without God. Hence, John of the Cross chose 2 Corinthians 6:10 as his favorite Biblical text, "Having nothing, yet having all." The sense of one's nothingness is for mystics a correlate of the reality of God. Sartre's "draining one's own self dry with the sense of thirst" and John Donne's "with a great, sober thirst my soule attends" have the same structure. They lack only the same substance.

The thirst of existential history testifies only to man's nothing-

[1] *The Mind's True Itinerary*, Ch. IV, section 2.

ness. Man is "a clown dancing on the edge of an abyss." (Balzac) Although the tragedy of the tight-rope walker may have the aspect of a comedy, actually, it is "a sickening struggle, eye to eye, with death." (Cocteau) Man is in the position of "a cat on a hot tin roof!" His situation is untenable and he has the irrepressible desire to leap.

This leap will be a leap in the dark only in the sense that one does not see where he is going. But the very untenability of the darkness out of which one leaps, is in itself what the early mystical theologian of Christianity, the Pseudo-Dionysius, called the "ray of darkness for the understanding." Eckhart called this darkness "potential sensitivity." There is a luminousness about the "dark night of the soul" which the existentialist undergoes when he assumes his vocation as the shepherd of being. The teetering on the edge of the abyss, the giddiness of the spirit which comes with the contemplation of one's possible nothingness, far from its being a condition of spiritual opacity, produces what Marcel seems to be willing to call "the fetal moment of consciousness." This darkness is a darkness you could call dark, a nothingness you could call nothing, "provided you called vacant and empty the silent and lifeless terrain in front of a mobilized army, or peaceful the vestibule to a powder magazine, or quiet the spillway under the locks of a dam" (Faulkner)—or childless a pregnant woman.

In this "fetal moment" of existential darkness, however, even the existentialists appear to compromise the discipline of thirst and leap into philosophically unauthorized promises of satisfaction. Sartre and Camus leap, find that the water does not support them, but find at the same time that their very thrashing about holds them up. Absurdity, meaninglessness—that is, nothingness, has the last word, except for their heroic effort to negotiate a meaningful life even after the realization that it is impossible. Jaspers, on the other hand, leaps and has a vision of a transcendent metaphysical reality which has not yet arrived but to which he pins his hope as a shipwrecked seaman to the mirage of a rescue ship. Jaspers accepts the meaninglessness and lack of support in the world as a clue to a support beyond the world and develops a metaphysic based on a kind of philosophical faith—what the fifteenth-century German mystic Nicholas of Cusa called the *docta ignorantia* or learned ignorance.

The so-called "Christian existentialists" leap, thrash around, sense the depth of what Kierkegaard calibrated as 70,000 fathoms of water, but miraculously feel their hand strike against an object, a Real Presence outside themselves, which has come to them as a life raft to a drowning man. That presence is God turning to man in Jesus Christ. Here they cease being existentialists, devoted to the encounter with nothingness, and become Christians. They cease living in existential history except in the sense that a Christian man is always both a nihilist and a man of faith, always testing his gratitude for salvation by his temptation not to trust. Kierkegaard adopts the Lutheran faith, Berdyaev the Eastern Orthodox, Marcel the Roman Catholic.

Heidegger, of all the existentialists, maintains the discipline of thirst, the patient waiting for God, the penultimate mysticism. *Holzwege* may have been for Barth paths in the woods which lead nowhere. But for Heidegger there is philosophical wisdom in knowing as the woodsman does, lost at night upon his *Holzwege*, that one must stop and wait for the coming of light. Heidegger builds his entire concept of truth around this principle, a principle also central to mysticism. To have truth is not to grasp the real object; it is to let the object be. To let the object be is not a situation of indifference. On the contrary, existence is between being and thought, is *inter-esse*. In this way, existence is *interested* being. But existential interest is not a kind of subjectivity which disfigures objective truth as any knave reshapes a wax nose, to suit his face. In the presence of the ultimate reality one thinks as it is said one thinks in the presence of Lehmbruck's sculpturing, not "of it" but "with it." God is not object but "inject." One *lives* God, or better, "is lived by God." (Meister Eckhart) Existential truth catches up in it, in a non-theological way, the force of the Hebrew *amen*. In the presence of an object which it cannot grasp it simply confesses, "So let it be."

III. ON LETTING GOD BE

There seems to be a philosophical genuineness about this procedure that is not present in some other existential results. If to be in Christ is the Christian truth, then, of course, Heidegger is not in the Christian truth. But is he not faithful to the shepherding of being as a philosopher when he refuses to close the existential itinerary in a meeting with a false God, or to quench his thirst at an inauthentic fountain, or to write a "Christian philosophy"? As Arthur Koestler has said, "The ultimate truth is penultimately always a falsehood." The existential philosopher, mystic only in the penultimate sense, is willing to be damned to *laissez-faire Dieu*, as the seventeenth-century French mystics put it, to "let God be."

Existential history is the refusal to name the gods, linked with the apprehension that nothing is more important than to know who God is. Hence, when existentialism is an atheism, it is not so in any customary sense. It may be a tragic atheism as Nietzsche's or an insolent atheism as Sartre's or a reverent atheism as Heidegger's. In every case, however, it is an open confession by the man as philosopher that he does not have access to the authentic God beyond all inauthentic half-gods. These atheisms differ when one considers the philosopher as a man and his capacity to live without a solution to the most important existential question, the question about the ultimate meaning of being. But at least this is patent among the existentialists: not one of them rejoices when he announces that "God is dead," not even Sartre. While Sartre concludes from the death of God that all men are free, this freedom is a burden and a sickness like the freedom of an autumn leaf unbound to a living branch or the freedom of a child away from his home. I do not believe it is an inordinate rationalization of the existential position to claim that even atheism is "a ray of darkness for the understanding" which tutors us in the risk of yielding to inauthentic gods. *Laissez-faire Dieu* is the highest confession of mysticism in its penultimate form. It is a waiting for the God beyond all gods (Dionysius, Eckhart, Tillich) who, if he is to have a name, must make it known himself.

Most of the theological criticisms of mysticism which are to be found among theologians are directed against non-historical mysticism which is vulnerable to pantheistic and quietistic tendencies. These criticisms, however, are inapplicable to mysticism in its historical, penultimate expression. John Wesley, for instance, testified that he almost suffered shipwreck on mysticism. He was referring, however, to ultimate mysticism and not to its existential, historical, penultimate stage.

Dietrich Bonhoeffer, however, rightly warns of one shoal on which even this penultimate mysticism could founder. It is the temptation to make existential yearning for ultimate meaning, or the sense of tragedy without it, the human presupposition for Christian faith. It is the desire to turn the existential philosophy into the apologetic handmaiden of the Christian faith. Such a synthesis of existentialism to the Christian faith sets up the feeling of the need of God as the necessary first step toward appropriation of the knowledge of God. In this method, the philosophy is reduced to an ancillary of the Christian faith and the church militant is on its way toward becoming "the church litigant." (G. B. Shaw)

The Christian uses of existentialism are rather what the original existentialists, Pascal and Kierkegaard, saw them to be: attacks upon Christendom. Existentialism is helping the contemporary world enter into a kind of penultimate mysticism which exposes the poverty of man when he sees no ultimate in history. This self-knowledge is a cultural assault of the greatest significance upon the presuppositions of much of popular Christianity, against its banalities and what Nietzsche called its "half-stoical and smiling indifference to the seriousness of the faith." Regrettably, offense is still taken to be the best defense, even in theology. Hence, almost before this laicized mysticism has had a chance to prick the side of the church, the church has turned it back upon the world in offensive apologetics and missionary theology. Meanwhile, the world in its unquenched thirst and its unconsummated itinerary offers up existential history as a "ray of darkness" for the guidance even of the church. As Hölderlin said,

> Who follows sacred callings like a trade
> His face is false and cold and dead, *as are*
> *His Gods!*

One needs to be reminded, as Koestler has reminded us in *Darkness at Noon*, that "the ultimate truth is penultimately always a falsehood." It may come as a surprise to learn, however, that Bonhoeffer endorses *"remaining deliberately* in the penultimate." By doing so he believes we may "point all the more genuinely to the ultimate, which God will speak in his own time (though indeed even then through a human mouth)," that is, through history.[1]

---

[1] *Ethics*, S. C. M. Press, 1955, pp. 84, 85.

CHAPTER
5

HISTORY IN GOD'S ABSENCE

EXISTENTIAL history is a history of the pockets of meaninglessness which threaten the hope for an ultimately meaningful world. A history with gaps might be tolerable if it were simply the transitory superstructure of a solidly continuous natural world beneath. But when the insolidity of nature itself becomes apparent, as it does in modern science, the question about history is reopened with a new urgency, for one sees his own existence is at stake in the answer. Man's historical consciousness has surely been quickened by the understanding of his place in the world, exposed by modern science. Quite fortuitously, selfhood has been brought to taut awareness.

The main ingredient in this awakening has been the realization of the self-determining character of his freedom. The rational acts of modern man, so probing and so gratifying, come up against an order of reality which is impervious simply to a rational act. In that collision man feels a tension in his being which existentialism has identified with a self more basic than rationality, that is, with freedom. Hereafter, the rationality of man cannot be presumed to be exhausted in acts of scientific and logical transparency. There is a form of rationality in which the reason takes its clues from another dimension, the rationality of freedom engaged in the struggle for an authentic life. That level of reality is history, and the rational acts informed and executed on the basis of that level are known as acts of the historical reason. The life of the historical reason is "the mind's true itinerary," a quasi-mystical quest for a reality which never appears. Existential mysticism is the authentic life of the historical reason because of the courage with which it protracts its refusal to invoke its freedom to choose a god lest an idol be embraced. That refusal is known in our time as atheism, which is history in God's absence.[1]

Considering its reputation for atheism, existentialism's contribution to an understanding of God is not the least of its achievements. The theistic help which existentialism gives is largely confined to the dimension of existential history, which means nothing positive is being said about God by existentialists. On the contrary, their vocation is to witness to the death of God. That witness is a form of existential history, for it is the sense of a mortal wound in humanity's ongoing life. It is the realization that there is nothing apparently ultimate in history. Not that we cannot live meaningfully in such a history. We can salvage little caches of meaning to delight us and support us intermittently. One cannot say world history is devoid of meaning simply because meaning does not apparently have the last word. Existential history nevertheless has the function of confessing that if there is no living God, death may have the last word and history would have no ultimacy. There would be no future in history. The paratactic wounds in history, when left unknit, are signs in the process of life which already forecast that finally life is meaningless. Without God nothing is possible.

I. ATHEISM AND DEICIDE

Several generations of Christians have been made anxious by Nietzsche's announcement that "God is dead." Contemporary

---

[1] Cf. Stanley Romaine Hopper, "On the Naming of the Gods in Hölderlin and Rilke," *Christianity and the Existentialists*, edited by Carl Michalson, Scribners, 1956, ch. 8.

existentialists, by taking up the cry, have renewed the anxiety of
the church. "We believe in God!" the Christians assert, and then
dismiss existentialism as atheistic. What is rarely understood about
existentialism is that its obituary at the grave of God is meant to
be the testimony of a witness. Deicide has been committed. Someone has failed to let God be. Existentialism is not the murderer.
It is simply the witness to the crime. As Nietzsche said, it is the
churches which are the tombs of God, and God is dead not because he never existed, but because his worshippers have killed him
with belief. The very manner of the church's credence is the
murder weapon. Christian believers have constructed theistic
world-views where decisions were required. They have made God
in man's image without being correct about man in the first place.
The effect has been to destroy in man the consciousness of "vertical transcendence." (Camus) If an atheist, therefore, is one who
announces that no God could be believed as man believes him
and survive, then existentialism is atheistic.

Luther was an atheist judged by that standard. Confronted by
the tendency of the medieval church to Aristotelianize God,
Luther had no alternative. "According to Aristotle," as Ortega y
Gasset has said, "God does nothing but think about thought—
which is to convert God into an intellectual, or, more precisely,
into a modest professor of philosophy." To speak of the God of
Abraham, Isaac and Jacob in terms so bloodless is deicide, and
Luther witnessed the crime. Existentialism at least conserves
Luther's sense of a shudder at the thought that without God
nothing is possible.

Judged by the same standard, Dietrich Bonhoeffer was an
atheist. The fragments of his writings reveal his distress over the
religious man's mechanization of God. The religious man uses
God as "a working hypothesis," a *deus ex machina*, a miraculous
way of escape from the perplexities of life. When he does, he is
out of joint with his time, for the world has "come of age." It no
longer "needs" God in the world, whether in morals, politics or

science. Religious men *want* to need Him, however, so they make themselves weak in the world in order to validate their claim to God's existence as the sole power in the world. This is deicide, and Bonhoeffer witnessed it when he said,

> God is teaching us that we must live as men who can get along very well without Him. . . . Before God and with Him we live without God. God allows Himself to be edged out of the world and on to the cross. God is weak and powerless in the world, and that is exactly the way, the only way, in which He can be with us and help us. . . . The world come of age was an abandonment of a false conception of God, and a clearing of the decks for the God of the Bible, who conquers power and space in the world by His weakness.[1]

If atheism is a witness to the death of God by murder, then Rudolf Bultmann is also an atheist. God is set aside, according to Bultmann, not by denying him but by affirming him in the wrong way. Ironically, the theologians are the class of people most likely to commit deicide. To that extent Franz Overbeck was right at the turn of the century to charge the theologians with violation of the third commandment. In their scientific way of talking about God they profane God, as psychologists profane love who describe it in abstraction from acts of love. In his *Commentary on Genesis* Luther said that the sin of Adam was not the act of eating the forbidden fruit. It was allowing himself to be drawn into an objective discussion about whether God should have set up such a prohibition. "To talk about God scientifically is not only an error and a delusion; it is a sin. . . . To talk about God existentially means to accept His claim upon us. . . . God can never be seen from the outside. When the world tries to do so, it leaves itself godless."[2]

It is true that there is not a single existentialist who affirms that God is *necessary*. Some call that atheism. Others regard it as the

[1] *Prisoner for God*, Macmillan, 1953, p. 164.
[2] *Glauben und Verstehen*, Tübingen, 1933, Vol. I, pp. 27 and 33.

way to let God "be." The consequence is that some existentialists believe in God and some deny him. But the same quality of passionate personal involvement is present in each position. For if God were necessary, you could neither believe nor deny him. He would be a fate requiring submission. All existentialists agree in affirming that God is *possible,* some by their devotion (Marcel and Berdyaev), some by their metaphysical wistfulness (Heidegger and Jaspers), and some by their very rebellion against him (Camus and Sartre). It is these rebels among the existentialists who bring upon themselves the charge of atheism. One would be a fool to try to purvey their atheism as something completely palatable. But one would be irresponsible not to see something in it more suggestive of the resurrection of God than in some more confident avowals of God's existence.

Even in the blatant atheists among the existentialists, God is real in life although repudiated. For God is what is known as a "limit" or "boundary." Hence, Sartre who denies God also affirms that man is the futile desire to become God. Man is a being who is "in himself" and "for himself." He is sheer facticity, impacted in this present world. But he is project, too, invoked to move beyond his present posture. When the gap between what he is (in himself) and what he ought to be (for himself) is overcome, and he becomes "in and for himself," he will either be God or dead. To accept these limits for his life is for man the most significant act of existential realism. It is his redemption from what Augustine called the sin of pride. For it is *superbia* when a man considers himself as "in-and-for himself."[3] Therefore, one must learn to live and die, and being man, refuse to be God. (Camus)

There are two forms of atheism, then. Existentialism illustrates both, and no theology which loves life can afford to by-pass the judgment resident in each. There is the atheism which witnesses the affirmations of the pious that God exists. Seeing that they refer to a being whose absence would not reduce their history to nothing,

[3] *de Trinitate* XII, 11.

existentialism cries out "deicide!" And there is the atheism which, while denying God, nevertheless finds him setting the limits of life. "The absence of God moves about here with the intimacy of a presence." (Gustav Thibon) Thus, among the existentialists God causes the curses of men to praise him, like the character in Camus' *The Fall*, who unwittingly disperses the "café atheists" by his profane but passionate allusions to deity.

II. WHY GOD DOES NOT APPEAR

There is no way of affirming God from within existential history. The existentialists, mainly known for their transcriptions from existential history, put one question prior to the question about the possibility of God. That is the question about the possibility of history. Since the time of Immanuel Kant, historical matters have been given priority over metaphysics. Idealism from Hegel to Collingwood set its metaphysical questions within the framework of history. Positivism from Feuerbach and Marx to modern historicism gave the questions about the ultimate reality of history precedence over the questions about Ultimate Reality in itself. Kant may have initiated that whole modern movement. When Kant spread out before him what he regarded as the main issues for philosophy, he enumerated the problems of knowledge, morals, and immortality. A second look at these problems uncovered a common denominator. One can see it for oneself in the way Kant phrased the problems. "What can I know? What ought I do? What may I hope?" He found these questions reducible to a single question: "What am I?" or "What is man?" His answers to these questions were conclusions respecting the finitude of man's life. The existentialists, unlike the idealists and the positivists, pin their own destinies to the questions they raise. Kant's formulation in their hands becomes more querulous. "Am I?" they ask. And if I am, "why am I something and not nothing?" (Heidegger) The medieval mystic Hugh of St. Victor once phrased a similar question. "Why then, my God, have you created me, unless you wished me to exist rather than not to?"[1] The intention in Hugh's question is identical to the intention in Heidegger's. It is only the substance that is different. Radicalized in this way, philosophical anthropology which Kant made central was transmuted into a kind of secularized theology. The question about God's existence always stands to be reopened when man raises in a radical way the question about the possibility of history. Existentialism preoccupies itself with man and observes that man does not have within his history the conditions for a future. That observation opens the door to theology and the surmise about a possibility for ultimacy in history which is at the limit of man's withering flesh.

The method of handling the question about God is significantly affected by the way the question arises. Existential history suggests God in much the same way hunger suggests food. The idea of God constructed under these conditions is not, therefore, a development of the idea of existence in general. Kierkegaard felt the impossibility of this transition from existence to God so keenly, he refused to consent that God exists. "God does not exist," he claimed; "He is eternal."[2] This was not to be taken as a blasphemy, however. It was intended as a prophetic restriction upon the idolatries present in well-intentioned references to deity. For "existence" means "to stand from," which is radical contingency. God in the prophetic tradition stands from nothing but himself: he does not exist. "Existence" can also mean "to stand beyond," which is likewise radical contingency. But God has nothing beyond him to inspire a self-transcending reach so that one cannot say God exists.

The traditional western tactic of proving God's "existence," therefore, is vexed by existential history. Proofs for God should start from something faintly resembling God. An object known should have some correspondence with the knowledge of it. But

[1] *Soliloquy on the Earnest Money of the Soul*, Marquette University Press, 1956, p. 23.
[2] *Concluding Unscientific Postscript*, tr. by David F. Swenson and Walter Lowrie, Princeton University Press, 1944, p. 296.

existential history exposes the absence of God in history when it characterizes existence in a way that makes existence inapplicable to God. Does not God exist? Existence needs a first cause, a prime mover, a supreme good. Is not a first cause arrived at by tracing back through a linear series of causes to the first member in the series? To these traditional questions existential history reports the experience of the *lack* of just such continuity in the reality of existence—the cracks in nature and the gaps between events. There is no way back to God through history. Then, may not God be regarded as the whole series of causes and effects, not simply the first in the series? That would be pantheism. Considering the roughly segmented character of history and nature, it would be pantheism of a very peristaltic sort. Evolutionary theisms such as S. Alexander's nevertheless pursue that suggestion, allowing that the fissures in nature and history are experienced by God as God's own process of actualization. In that case, it could be said that "God exists," stretching out beyond himself through some *nisus* in his being toward higher self-realization.

Classical theisms do not accommodate to existential limitations so easily. God is not thought by them to be the first reality in a linear series. If he were, Karl Heim would be quite justified in charging their proofs with idolatry. They would be setting God up as an object within the conditions of existence, and God does not "exist." In classical theism, however, God is not the first in a linear series. He is the apex of an ontological pyramid. Between his primacy and all other levels of reality there is a chasm unbridgeable from the side of man. As Thomas Aquinas affirmed, God is not *primus inter pares*, the first among equals. He is in a genus of which he is the sole member. He is in a class by himself.

From the moment the theists begin to express their thoughts about God, they do so by analogies drawn from existence. Do these analogies escape the limitations which existential history finds in existence? Locating God in the ontological pyramid may deliver God from confusion with contingent realities. Does the language which signifies God escape that confusion? Strictly speaking, that is the intention of analogical reasoning. To designate God as first cause does not mean God *is* a first cause, but that he is *like* a first cause. God is to man as a father is to a son: that is the form of analogical reasoning. It does not say God *is* a father. Analogical reasoning is a less cautious form of predication than predication by negation, because it does not say simply what God is not. God is in some sense a first cause and in some sense a father, even though he is not really either. Analogy is nevertheless a form of the mystical *via negativa* which is designed to protect the onto-logical gap between God and history. Analogies speak of God in such a way as to distinguish what one says from what God is without separating what one says from what God is.

The language of existential history testifies to the same thing about God that classical theism does: God is not apparently in history. God does not exist. The difference is that classical theism formulated its judgment differently. Existential history provides no evidence that God is there. Classical theism, however, says God is not apparently in history because he is the very Possibility of history. Existentialism announces that without God nothing is possible. Classical theism says that with God everything is possible. These affirmations are opposite sides of the same coin. Man exists, but he is not possibility. Man simply *has* possibility. But God *is* Possibility. God is the Possible one. That means God is the being who is the possibility of everything else.

The phrase "the possibility of" is a syntactical symbol for the structure that relates God and history. "Possibility" is not employed here as philosophy is accustomed to doing it. No scholastic would use the term "possible" with reference to the being of God, because for scholasticism "possible" connotes "potential" or the lack of actuality. Process philosophy and other theistic naturalisms use the term today for the very same reason scholasticism rejects it. Process philosophy is developed on the assumption that God is in some sense always in the process of actualizing his being. With reference to the knowledge of God, scholastics and naturalists alike would use the term "possible," for to say God is possible simply means he is "conceivable" or that the idea of God is a non-contradictory idea.

"Possible" in this discussion about the reality of God has neither of these meanings. Rather, it takes on the coloration which the early fathers of the church believed they found in Greek philosophy. The contemporary philosopher Martin Heidegger has revived the meaning for today. To do so, he has dived into a very deep terminological sea for a verbal pearl too lustrous for most theological vocabularies. There is a kind of being, he claims, which must be called *das Mögliche*, the possible one. It is the being which is the very power of being, conferring on all reality its possibility. It is the "stillen Kraft des Möglichen," "the secret power of the possible one."[3]

The term should not be unfamiliar to the student of the Bible. One can test one's comprehension of it by employing it as a synonym of the Greek word, *dunatos*. Reread the Magnificat supplanting *dunatos* with *das Mögliche* and you will see what Heidegger means: "He who is possible has done great things for me, and holy is his name." (Luke 1:49) Or read the popular verse, Matthew 19:26, with the same substitution: "With God all things are *possible*." This word embraces a meaning which shifts ontological concern from its customary preoccupation. Ontology traditionally has been prepossessed by considerations of the intrinsic nature of being. An ontology on the base of existential history will be taken up with the *operations* of being and with the *structure* sustained in the relations of being.

The ontological structure implied in the syntax, "the possibility of," is intended in both theology and existential history. It is the symbolic way of saying that the affirmation of the reality of God

---

[3] *Platons Lehre von der Wahrheit*, p. 57, 58; cf. also *Sein und Zeit*, pp. 143, 144; *Vom Wesen des Grundes*, pp. 37 ff., and *Einführung in der Metaphysik*, pp. 150, 151.

cannot be deduced from the conditions of history. Judged by everything that exists, God does not apparently exist. Whereas existential history bases its judgment on the apparent absence of God, classical theism bases its judgment on the necessity for God's apparent absence. As the possible one, God is hidden at the base of all the possibilities in history which are sustained by him. This sense of ontological structure motivated Pascal to say that "every religion which does not affirm that God is hidden, is not true."[4]

The intellectual sources of this view concerning the historical absence of God root back in certain emphases in Pythagoras, Plato, and Aristotle. Pythagoras had a pedagogical trick for putting this point across with his students. He would sketch out numbers in the sand: "one . . . two . . . three . . . four . . . five." Then he would challenge his students to tell him which was the "greatest" number. Like students today, his were prone to give priority to magnitudes and hastily concluded, "Five!" There the teacher had them. For, as he would say, what would "five" be without "one." "Five" is, after all, only five "ones," and "one" is the source and possibility of all other numbers. That means the difference between one and five is not simply quantitative but qualitative. "Possibility of" puts "one" in a class by itself. It has nothing in common with other numbers. e. e. cummings' "if everything happens that can't be done" could be decoded by Pythagoreanism:

> there's nothing as something as one
> one hasn't a why or because or although.

Plato, the first great philosophical theist, may also have presupposed Pythagoras when he gave hints of this qualitative structure between the irreducible and history in his "idea of the good." "The idea of the good" was regarded by Plato as the source, the possibility of all good, truth, and beauty, and of all existence. As such, it was believed to be "on the other side of essence and

[4] *Pensées*, fragment 584.

existence." It is transcendent, that is, apparently absent in history. As transcendent, the idea of the good by Plato's own testimony has nothing in common with history.[5]

Aristotle employed the same kind of thinking in his concept of the *arche*, the beginning or source. What has the source of motion in common with moving things? Nothing. The source is rather the possibility of motion. But it is that possibility, said Aristotle, "not as an immanent part."[6] It was within such patterns of intellectual clarity that the early Christian theists formed their deep insights about the God of Abraham, Isaac, and Jacob, and the God and Father of our Lord Jesus Christ. God is the great monad, they believed, who because he is the source and possibility of history cannot be there as an immanent part of history.

At the very same time that *arche* thinking with its concept of transcendence was being offered to theologians, another form of thinking in the Greek world was being offered but rejected by early Christianity. The fact that the alternative existed and that the church chose one rather than the other is enormously instructive for the importance attached to this particular theistic formulation. Stoicism, Hellenism, and Gnosticism were ready to supply Christianity with a principle of historical immanence in their concept of the *logos*. The Stoics were claiming that everything has logos and is to that degree divine. The Hellenistic Jew, Philo, was claiming that between God and history is a principle of wisdom which is neither God nor history, but a third thing called *logos* which brings the two together because it is ingredient in both. The Gnostics claimed that at creation God permitted a divine *logos*, a spiritual wisdom, a fragment of the fulness of the Godhead, to be slipped into the envelope of human flesh, its purpose being to accelerate the return of man to God.

Now it is true that the early theologians adopted the language of *logos*. It would be wrong to assume, however, that they meant

[5] *Republic* 509; *Phaedo* 97c-99c.
[6] *Metaphysics* 1013a.

by *logos* what Stoicism, Hellenism, and Gnosticism meant by it. There are very convincing grounds for observing that the early fathers, while choosing the language of *logos*—for whatever reasons, apologetic or otherwise—infused into the term the meaning *arche* formerly embraced. Most noteworthy among the so-called *logos* theologians was Clement of Alexandria. Why then did he insist, commenting on Jesus' command to be perfect "*as* your Father in heaven is perfect," "We do not say as the Stoics do impiously that virtue in man and in God is the same."[7] Why did Justin Martyr reject the analogy of the relation of the *logos* to God as rays to the sun, with their evident qualitative kinship?[8] It was a favorite Philonic analogy. And why did Irenaeus say, "God who sent forth the intellect is separate from it, and the intelligence separate from Him,"[9] except that he desired a sharp rejection of the Gnostic motif? These early fathers, while choosing the language of *logos*, had chosen the meaning of *arche* and had thus saved for Christian thinking the meaning of God as "the possible one" and the meaning of history as a realm of impossibility without God.

The later fathers were quite aware of the importance of this decision for the Christian faith. Theodore of Mopsuestia wrote, "What possible relation can exist between one who is eternal and another who at one time was non-existent and came into existence? . . . (They are) separated from each other and the gulf between them is unbridgeable."[10] Chrysostom wrote, "So great is the interval between man and God as no language can at all express."[11] And Nestorius wrote, "The Maker is in every way other than that which is made."[12] These were classical Christian theism's ways of saying that God does not exist, because he is the Possibility of existence. If God is the being who holds all history in his sustain-

---

[7] *Misc.* VII, xiv.
[8] *Dialogue with Trypho,* 128, 3.
[9] *Against Heresies* II, xiii, 4.
[10] *Commentary on the Nicene Creed.*
[11] *On the Statues* iii, 19.
[12] *The Bazaar of Heraclides.*

ing hand, there is no possibility within history for adequately describing him or even adducing his reality. God is apparently absent in history. Existentialism claims this on the basis of its poignant sense that the ultimate verdict of history will be on the side of nothingness. Christian theism claims it on the conviction that what is impossible with history is possible with God who cannot be "an immanent part of" history because he is the transcendent "possibility of" history.

The most prodigious critique of classical theism is found today among the philosophers and theologians influenced by the process views of Alfred North Whitehead. Mainly two deficiencies are brought to light by the process theisms. The classical view has depicted a God who is both too static and too transcendent. Unfortunately, theology has inherited its notion of a static God from the same Greek ontology which supplied it with the key to its view of transcendence. When process thinkers refute the static tendency, they sound consistent with the Biblical view of a God who lives and suffers. Temporal connotations were utterly alien to the theism of the Greeks, but the God of the Bible seems to have some kind of history of his own.

Process philosophy, however, calls for the abandonment of the transcendence of God along with the abandonment of all static references to God. In doing so, it creates a kind of philosophical package deal concerning which theologians who have commerce with philosophy should be on guard. The view in which this twin rejection occurs is called "pan-en-theism." Pan-en-theism is a very prudent philosophical safeguard against the excessive immanence of pantheism. Where pantheism identifies the whole process of history with God, pan-en-theism attempts to show how history can be in God without God being in history, at least as an immanent part. Philosophies of immanence have expressed God's involvement in history by identifying him in some way with the process of history. Process philosophy achieves the same end but avoids the *logos* heresy by re-defining the structure of God's relation to existence. God influences the process of history and is present *to* it, but he is not *in* the process. The process is in him. In this respect, process thinking is in direct continuity with classical Christian theism.

At one signal point, however, the process theology breaks with the meaning of transcendence. For in pan-en-theism, while God is transcendent in his primordial nature, in his consequent nature God is transcended by history. The being of God burgeons with the decisions of man. That means that at least in one aspect of his nature God can no longer be regarded as "the Possible one." He is a possibility alongside other possibilities. Human history becomes in some sense the possibility of God, so that Whitehead, the father of the view, believed it is as true to say man creates God as to say God creates man. For whatever reasons, whether the democratic prejudice of the west or the nature orientation in the language of contemporary scientific philosophies, the sovereign of the universe in this philosophy becomes in some sense an epiphenomenon of the voting power of man. In this view one may say "God exists." In so saying, however, process theism unwittingly endorses the death of God by binding his fate to the fortunes of history.

III. HISTORICAL "PROOFS" FOR GOD

All proofs for the existence of God have one chastening characteristic in common. The reality they aim to demonstrate is no less absent from history after the proof than before it. Was Immanuel Kant right, then? Is it true that cogent thoughts do not produce concrete realities? No theistic demonstration has been devised which successfully carries off the radar-like pretensions implied in Q. E. D. When the proof has been projected, no report returns to show that the reality has been engaged. What may seem to the reader a calamitous and anti-climactic exposé of the emptiness of proofs for God could actually have the very opposite meaning. If God is the Possible one who just by virtue of the power of his being as transcendent source remains inaccessible to the existential process, the proof of such a being is precisely in his historical absence. Existential history verifies the absence. Theology illuminates the confession to God's absence by calling it a testimony not to his unreality, but to the structure in his relationship to history. The best proof of a God who is by definition hidden would be the inability of the proof to produce him.

Another value in proofs for God is less facetious but just as oriented to existential history. It is philosophically unfair to conclude that proofs which do not strike their targets have no value. One must not dissociate from the proof the concern with which one takes his aim. The question about the possibility of God's reality is unanswerable within history. It would be unwise, however, to neglect the innuendo in the fact that the question is so unavoidable. "The heart has reasons the head knows not of." Not to transcribe the reasons of the heart is philosophically irresponsible. Pascal's confession gives credence to the historical reason, it does not simply express a failure of philosophic nerve. One should be able to say of the philosopher without provoking laughter what Samuel Beckett has Hamm say in *Endgame*. There is "a heart in his head." It is true that a fully Biblical view of the method of understanding God would require the emphases in Pascal and Anselm to be linked together. Pascal made the head responsible to the heart. Anselm made the heart responsible to the head. The Bible makes heart and head organic to each other. In his very theoretical proofs for the existence of God, however, Anselm was right to show that the fool who said in his heart, "There is no God," played the fool by denying in his heart what was undeniable in his head.

There is a suggestive kinship between what Pascal called the "wager" and what Charles Peirce called the "neglected argument" for God. The kinship is precisely at the point of the organicity of head and heart which is the historical character of the reason. What if the theoretical reason cannot know whether or not there is a God? One is left with a gamble. One ought to wager, Pascal concluded, and the safer bet is that there is a God. Peirce also believed that the personal and social benefits accruing from belief in God had not been seriously enough seized by philosophers. The sheer pragmatic value of the belief, he claimed, should throw more weight on the side of God's possible reality than on the side of disbelief.

The strong conviction that reality is not rounded out unless God be acknowledged is a type of "proof" which does not require *quod erat demonstrandum* or a punctured target. It moves in an atmosphere of personal concern and sense of gratitude which bespeaks prevenient reality. Descartes called his proofs for God *Meditations*. Anselm prayed the prologue to his proof for God. The entire theism of Nicholas of Cusa was in the form of prayer. These knew they presupposed the reality they wished to demonstrate. All efforts to make the absent God seem real are more impressive for their passionate concern than for their theoretical result. But that is what would be expected of a reality which remains the hidden source and possibility even of the efforts to make him visible.

Contemporary phenomenological philosophy has helped to regularize the insights in methods which presuppose what they demonstrate. Not that phenomenology thinks about God. Phenomenology is the philosophy of what appears, of phenomena; and God, being the limit of existence, the possibility of history, by definition "does not appear." (Husserl) Generally speaking, however, the phenomenologist believes two conditions are basic to the occurrence of knowledge, the objective and the subjective. The subject, who is the knower, reaches out toward the object, which is what is known. The object supplies the possibility of its being grasped. But knowledge does not take place except as the knower "passionately loves" the object, stretching out toward it with his consciousness. The important point for our purposes here is that confirmation of a reality which is indicated in one's consciousness is not entirely dependent upon reaching the reality. There is theoretical validity and epistemological realism in the very stretching out. Existentialists have employed this phenomenological structure to safeguard their cognitive seriousness about subjective moods from the charge of mere subjectivism. Subjectivity can be truth, as Kierkegaard said, if pointing to objects is given the same kind of validity which touching them formerly enjoyed.

Phenomenology also attributes a very suggestive role to the object in the process of knowledge. The condition for the possibility of knowledge is in the object for man in much the same way nectar is in the flower for the bee. The acquisitive bee finds in the nectar the very wax by which he may construct the bins in which he stores the honey. Reality assumes a similar beneficence toward the knowing mind.

It is within this context that Max Scheler proposed his "proof for the unprovability of God."[1] Scheler, the philosopher of religion among phenomenologists, unlike Husserl, was willing to apply the method to questions about God. If the reality after which the proof is seeking is regarded as a personal God, he said, then God is indemonstrable. It is the property of a person to be able to conceal himself at will. No person is ever known except as he voluntarily reveals himself to the knower. If the God one would know is conceived as personal, then there is a kind of knowledge process in relation to divine reality which is never consummated apart from God's prior will to reveal himself. No proof for the existence of a personal God can be consummated without the initiative of the object of the proof.

If that be the case, Anselm could well have written about two fools and not simply one. There is the fool he identified who said, "There is no God," not knowing that, in Max Picard's words, "he must continually tear the *no* away from the *is*, but again and again the *no* is brought back by the *is* and is swallowed up by it."[2]

[1] *Vom Ewigen im Menschen*, Leipzig, 1921, pp. 632 ff.
[2] *The Flight from God*, tr. by M. Kuschitzky and J. M. Cameron, Regnery, 1951, p. 20.

But there is also the fool who says "God is," yet does not appreciate that "the possibility of" saying "God is" resides in the prevenient reality named "I am." As Origen once said to Celsus, one cannot seek God and find him without help from God.

A lingering question could disintegrate the entire effort at establishing God's reality. One might be brought to concede with some kind of heart-felt confidence that "there is a God." One might ask about God because one must, because some urgency in one's history requires it. One might guard the language of one's surmise against mere psychologism and wish-fulfillment by negative and analogical devices, conceding that God transcends the realities within man's grasp. One might even grant that everything one says or does by way of movement toward God had already begun in God's own movement toward man. But is one yet beyond the cracking dryness of abstraction and the chambered echo of a human question? Can one, by saying, "There is a God," remove suspicion from the claim that God, though absent, is, without somehow the grounds for saying, "*There* God is!"?

This candor accounts for two vigorous tendencies in theology today. It accounts for the rejection of natural theology and for the renewal of trinitarianism. Natural theology is dedicated to finding out something about God through realities other than God which are available to man, such as nature and history. No one who has navigated the ambiguities in these realities at the level of existential history with its cracks and paratactic gaps can any longer take much cheer from the promises of natural theology. And even if one were quite able by these independent methods to arrive at some reliable information about the deity, one no longer needs that kind of knowledge. The point is not whether one can find something out about God in nature but whether one can find *God* there.

"Surely if God is the creator, his creative spirit is in nature?" No man who knows God as the possible one can hear that pious, popular confusion without a cry of protest. No! God is in his creative spirit, but he is not in what exists on the basis of his creative spirit. God is present to nature and history; but he is not present in it. His presence is an absence, which is his absolute distinctiveness and transcendence. One must not perforate the line between the possible one and all that he makes possible. "The Divine power and light . . . is everywhere in Nature, yet Nature touches it not." (Jacob Boehme)

One might conceivably point to nature or history and say, "There *is* a God!" But one cannot point to either nature or history and say, "*There* God is." Were one to do so, both a fallacy and a heresy would result. There would be the logical fallacy of composition, lumping together indiscriminately the knowledge about God and the knowledge of God himself. And there would be the theological heresy of composition, holding that God's nature can be parcelled out and yet be integrally himself. God *is* not in nature or history. He is *their* possibility. His silence may be there, but not his speech. His hands and feet, perhaps, as Calvin said; but not his heart.

The doctrine of the Trinity affirms, however, that there is a place in history to which one may point with the assurance that "*There* God is." That place is Jesus Christ. The general knowledge available in nature and history, although it cannot produce the absent God, can strengthen the surmise that God is real. The special revelation which bears the name of Jesus Christ is the possibility for saying not simply that the absent God is real but that the absent God is present. The doctrine of the Trinity is the theological way of naming God and of elucidating how in Jesus Christ revealer and revelation are in some sense the same reality. Hereafter God is known not simply as "being" (*Sein*) but as "being there for us." (*Dasein*)

Not that Jesus Christ is the total revelation of God. He is the revelation of the total God. Where he is, God is. God whose absence in world history is witnessed by existential history is present at the point in history called Jesus Christ. Where that presence occurs, world history is transmuted, given an ultimate end which existential history reveals is everywhere absent. That is why where Jesus Christ is present, history has a future, for it is filled with ultimate possibility. At that presence, the wretchedness and wistfulness of existential history is overcome by "the new age" of eschatological history.

Since the advent of Jesus Christ, the question about God does not begin to do justice to what is known about him until it moves beyond the "proof" of his reality to the proclamation of his presence. The question of the reality of God has been suggested to theology by concerns that have only a penultimate relation to the Christian belief. And the ultimate truth is penultimately always a falsehood. One must, of course, deal with these concerns. They have the intention of the faith, even though they lack the substance and structure of the faith. But one must not court the illusion that the movement from the penultimate to the ultimate is smooth. That transition is evoked when the Christian witnesses to the presence of God in Christ. The sense of his presence makes the prior sense of his absence fully understandable for the first time, and makes the existential quandary over his absence quite superfluous. The God who is experienced as the absent God in existential history is experienced as the present God in the eschatological history which the Christian proclamation heralds. The God and father of Jesus Christ is a God whose reality is not simply being but being there for us; not simply an *ousia* but a *parousia*, a presence. That makes the Christian life a life lived in a history which has a future because it is lived *coram deo*, in the presence of God. From now on, as Roger Mehl has said, "the true propagators of atheism are . . . those who direct this doubt at the heart of the faithful: Is your god really interested in you, is your god really present?"[3]

---

[3] *La Condition du philosophe Chrétien*, Paris, 1947, p. 78.

PART TWO

ESCHATOLOGICAL HISTORY

"In His will is our eternal peace."

DANTE, *Paradise*, canto 3, lxxxv

"Revelation is not only an increment of knowledge but a new way of seeing everything, a new meaning and courage."

WILHELM HERRMANN, *Der Begriff der Offenbarung*, Giessen, 1887, p. 6.

WHERE God is present, existential history is given an end and life is caught up in eschatological history. Existential history reports life in a world where God is apparently absent and hope is a waning reality. That is why theology can find no finally adequate formulation of its convictions among existential motifs. For theology is built upon the witness of the Biblical faith in which existential hopelessness is continually being overcome by events which witness God's presence.

Existential history is a phenomenon in world history. Eschatological history, on the other hand, is a phenomenon in Biblical history where events which have finality give history the form of its existence. In Christ the beginning and the end, the *arche* and the *telos* of history occurs. World history comes to an end in the sense of being transcended by a higher history. Even Biblical history comes to an end. Henceforth, Jesus Christ is the source and possibility of a history where hopelessness is once and for all overcome. Jesus Christ is the form and the content of the event through which God now calls the world to decision, and by that call precipitates the new age of eschatological history.

Traditionally, eschatology has referred exclusively to "the last things," by which was meant the events occurring at the end of time—death, resurrection, and final judgment. Recently, however, eschatology has taken on another meaning. Ernst Troeltsch is largely responsible for initiating the trend. He has made the claim that "eschatology has nothing whatsoever to do with time."[1] What he meant was that eschatology refers to ends, to what is "in the

[1] The article entitled "Eschatologie" in *Religion in Geschichte und Gegenwart*, first edition.

145

last analysis" (*am Ende*). More Biblically oriented theologians who have seen "the end" in Christ have saved Troeltsch's meaning by expressing it in the dynamic categories of Biblical history. Eschatology has indeed to do with time, but it is not defined by time. The last moments of time do not define eschatology. Eschatology qualifies the last moments of time as well as all moments of time "as salt qualifies a dish of food." (Gogarten) Where Christ is present, there is the end.[2]

Christ is not the eschatological event because he will enter history at some last moment of time but because when he appears in history, history comes to an end in its old form and the last, the eschatological age begins. Only in that sense of the word is it meaningful that theologians say eschatology is not to be treated as the last chapter in theological textbooks; it is "the peg on which everything else hangs."[3] That sense of the word also supplies the clue to understanding contemporary theological references to eschatology which have seemed unhistorical in character. When Reinhold Niebuhr says the eschaton is "beyond history" he does not mean it is unhistorical. He means it is not a product of world history but the "end" of world history. When Rudolf Bultmann says "all history is swallowed up in eschatology" he does not mean eschatology has nothing to do with history. He means it is the event which gives all history its new point of beginning.

The Biblical faith taken as a whole is not unanimous respecting what constitutes the end of history. The Old Testament divides between prophetic and apocalyptic emphases. The prophets anticipated a renewal of the world. The apocalyptic writers anticipated its collapse, and the advent of a new world on its ruins. But the Old Testament is agreed in acknowledging that the end, whatever its form, has not come. The holy history conserved in the Old Testament is a history of divine promise and human

---

[2] Cf. the comprehensive essay by Hidenobu Kuwada in his book called *Understanding Theology*, Tokyo, 1939, pp. 189-215.
[3] Emil Brunner, *Vom Werk des heiligen Geistes*, p. 61.

unfulfillment. The New Testament is the record of divine fulfillment. The advent of Christ is expressed in utterly apocalyptic terms. The coming of Jesus heralds the end of the world. It was the genius of Johannes Weiss and Albert Schweitzer to have pointed this out. The New Testament faith is a thoroughly eschatological faith in which Christ is seen as the end of the world, the beginning of a new history.

While the New Testament is more apocalyptic in its eschatology than it is prophetic, it does not encourage cosmological inferences which are the hallmark of Old Testament apocalyptic. To speak of eschatological history descriptively in terms of changes in the circumstances of the world is to express in nature categories what is really only significant in history categories. Eschatology satisfies the question about the meaning of history; it does not gratify man's visual curiosity. Jesus, therefore, refused to calculate the time of the end: that was a technological consideration. (Luke 17:20 ff.) He refused to court the expectation of a cosmic miracle: no sign should be anticipated. (Mark 8:12)

The apostle Paul, who began his ministry in the expectation of a cosmologically defined apocalyptic, gradually reinterpreted the end as freedom from the old world of sin, death, and the law, achieved through the presence of God in Christ. In Paul's view the eschaton has come when a man ceases basing his life on the world and receives his existence from God through the event of Christ. The Johannine writings almost entirely abandon the cosmography of the apocalyptic view of the end, supplanting that with the vision of a new age already fulfilled in Christ. "Not that John denies the coming of Christ as an event, making it a process of the soul. Rather, he opens the eyes of the reader to the realization that the end has already occurred."[4]

The book of the Revelation is in some ways the most convincing testimony that eschatological history has begun in Christ. Luther

[4] Rudolf Bultmann, *Glauben und Verstehen*, Vol. I, Tübingen, 1933, p. 144. Cf. also his recent *The Presence of Eternity*, Harpers, 1958.

called the Revelation apocalyptic speculation with no Christ in it. It has more recently been seen that the Revelation needs to be restored to the Christian view in the same sense Luther restored Romans. For there Christ is the meaning, the purpose, the end of history—the first and the last. (1:17, 2:8, 22:13) Henceforth, because of him all future events have an end. This is not a new view for the New Testament. It is only one more way the New Testament has of saying "that eschatology and faith are identical."[5]

Eschatological history terminates the protracted hopelessness of existential history. Eschatological history is the revelation to world history that history has a future, a hope, an ultimate meaning. Christian theology, therefore, is primarily an exposition of history in its eschatological dimension, history as it is brought to an end by the presence of God in Jesus Christ. The issues and opportunities that arise from this claim must now be dealt with. What does it mean to say that God is present in Jesus Christ? (Chapter 6) If the history of Jesus Christ is the beginning of the end of history, if Christ is historical in a primarily eschatological sense, how does that knowledge affect one's understanding of the so-called historical Jesus? (Chapter 7) The resurrection of Christ is said to be the source as well as the "first-fruits" of the new age of eschatological history. How can the meaning of the resurrection be saved from the distortions which believers and unbelievers alike inflict upon it by their incredulous unhistorical methods of interpretation? (Chapter 8) If Christ as the end of history is an event which occurs in the past at a point in world history, how is it that the preaching of the church can make him present today as the source and possibility of a meaningful existence? (Chapter 9)

An answer to these questions should begin to demonstrate more clearly how the motifs of eschatological history fill the paratactic

[5] Heinz-Dietrich Wendland, Geschichtsanschauung und Geschichtsbewusstsein im Neuen Testament, Göttingen, 1938, pp. 53 and 56. Cf. Lynn Harold Hough's Introduction to The Revelation, The Interpreter's Bible, Abingdon, 1958.

gaps in existential history, how Christ becomes the hinge of history, dispersing despair with hope. The leap from existential to eschatological history is the distance spanned by Christ. A theology written within these historical categories should be able to speak in a medium in which the eschatological fulfillment may occur. Its propositions are not invitations to intellectual assent but invocations to a new form of existence, a new history. Its affirmations are based upon no claims to authority, because in history there are no authorities. The test of the validity of a history inheres in the luminousness which it confers upon life at the dark limit of the world's hopes.

CHAPTER
6

HISTORY IN GOD'S PRESENCE

THE difference between existential history and eschatological history is the presence of God. God's apparent absence does not mean he is unreal. What, then, is the character of the presence of a God who is apparently absent? The presence of God converts the meaning of his evident absence into hiddenness, and as Pascal has said, "every religion that does not affirm that God is hidden is not true."

Judged by Pascal's criterion Christianity is a true religion. The hiddenness of God is a recurrent refrain in the Old Testament. The New Testament reaffirms it and the major creeds of Christianity confess it. Common sense also supports it, and when a minority faith like Christianity finds its position being corroborated by common sense, it has real grounds for enthusiasm.

Pascal said, however, that "a religion that does not say why God is hidden is not instructive." (*Pensées*, Fr. 584) Why is God hidden? The Christian answer is that God is so completely and indivisibly God in his presence, he cannot but remain hidden. The Hebrew-Christian tradition means by the hiddenness of God the way God has his being. In our myopic vision we reach out to bring God into our perceptual and conceptual scope, but God remains hidden. Why? Because our vision is finite? No; he is hidden because he is God. In our astigmatic way we try to draw God into our range of vision, but we fail. Why? Because our vision is corrupt? No; God remains hidden because he is God. While it is true that we fail to see God when we are looking in a direction in which God does not dwell, it is still more true that his hiddenness is an attribute not of our inability to see him but of his being God. The hiddenness of God is not an accident of history but an attribute of deity.[1]

It is God's very way of life to be hidden. His hiddenness is *ex officio*. Not just a being among beings, he is the source and possibility of all other beings. A structure is therefore implied in his relation to reality which must be presupposed not only as the basis for understanding God but as a basis for understanding reality in general. The hidden God is the God who transcends all being as the possibility of being. His hiddenness, therefore, is an attribute of his responsibility as God. Like the anchor of a ship, if he were not hidden he would not be performing his function. The pre-Socratic philosopher Heraclitus put this truth quite aphoristically: "Invisible harmony—better than visible." When this meaning is entered into, philosophies of immanence and optical metaphors for God will be abandoned by Christian thought for identical reasons.

Nothing is ultimately possible in history without the knowledge of God's presence. Yet the knowledge of God's presence is not what is usually meant by an historical possibility. God is present in Jesus Christ as the event which gives history its end. The presence of God in Jesus Christ is renewed in history when the witnesses to his presence communicate that witness to their time. History needs nothing more imperatively than the knowledge that there is a reality named God which occupies a place no other being can occupy. There is an irreversible structure in life which says only God is God and only with him is history ultimately possible. Not to know that truth is a source of wretchedness for human history, for it is a boundary which frustrates the human striving to be as God. The very hiddenness intensifies the peril,

[1] Cf. John Dillenberger, *God Hidden and Revealed*, Muhlenberg, 1953.

allowing men to come up hard against the boundary of their humanity without knowing it is God at the limit. The first commandment, therefore, is not to be looked upon as a moral dictum, a live option posed for man to choose. It is a benevolent announcement about the character of reality. "Thou shalt have no other Gods." That stricture is not the whim of an oriental despot; it is the structure of reality itself. The Psalmist and the Apostle were right to delight in that law. It is a guidepost for the *homo viator*, marking out his way through history as a way of spiritual liberty so long as it does not transgress prerogatives reserved for God alone.

I. NEARNESS WITHOUT IMMANENCE

The doctrine of the hiddenness of God is an affirmation of the transcendence of God which bespeaks God's way of being present. It should not be looked upon, therefore, as a counsel of despair or a concession to human finitude. It intends to be a characterization of God himself. Because it keeps man from looking for God in the wrong place it performs a merciful service. Because it assures man that God's apparent absence does not mean his unreality, it fosters hope in history. The Christian faith does not settle for the identification of God as anything less than God himself, nor will it condone the violation of the structure that puts God first.

By now it should be clear that the transcendence of God does not mean God is very far away. Meister Eckhart was not inconsistent with the meaning of transcendence when he said in a sermon, "God is nearer to me than I am to my own self." Transcendence does not jeopardize the intention of immanence, which is simply to articulate the nearness of God. Philosophies of immanence overreach themselves by identifying God in some sense with the process of nature and history. In so doing, they do less than justice to the paratactic aspects of reality to which existential history testifies. To say God is transcendent is not to locate him at a great distance, however. The truth is that God is transcendent because he is so very near and not because he is so very far. To say God is transcendent is rather to specify the structure in the relation between God and history, to describe the *way* in which God is present.

The most obvious meaning in the structure of transcendence is that God is different from man. The transcendence of God is *qualitative*. It is true that in the Bible the language of analogy is employed to the point of anthropomorphism. Nevertheless, the reader of the Bible is never left in doubt about the structure which says "I am God and not a man." That means that when one predicates something of man which can also be said of God, he does not mean the same thing at all.

The holiness of God is an apt illustration of that. To say God is holy could be taken to mean he is morally superior to man, a quantitative distinction. This would scarcely exhaust the meaning of the holiness of God in the presence of which one feels himself up against God. God's holiness is a *mysterium tremendum* which fascinates man in such a way as to cause him to sense the gap between himself and God. "I am better than God is," Meister Eckhart once said with no sense of personal pride. For moral comparatives were rightly held by him to be ultimately inapplicable to God. God is, as the mystics say, *exlex*, that is, beyond the law. God is holy because his is the possibility of the law. The holiness is in the tremendous mystery in the power of his being as possibility. One is drawn toward God's holiness as toward a fascinating jewel or a fascinating person. He is never attracted without simultaneously being repelled by awe. Worshippers express this feeling when they bow their heads, conceding the gap that separates them from God. Sometimes that structure is felt so deeply, and the attraction and repulsion is so contradictory in one's being, one experiences the sense of the holy as a sickness. I know a student who every time he stood next to his girl friend in the dining hall felt nauseated. Why? Because she sickened him? Yes, quite literally. But not because she was a sickening person. Quite to the contrary, she was so very desirable that when he sensed her tremendous mystery he was simultaneously attracted and repelled, and the contradiction within him was experienced as nausea. Little wonder, then, that every time Saint John of the Cross had a mystical vision of God he vomited.

God is God and man is man. Between these two realities there is a gulf fixed. It is desirable to refer to God's transcendence not only as qualitative, but as *spatial* if by spatial transcendence is meant not distance but distinctness. God is distinct from man as the spaces on a map or a checkerboard are distinct from each other. This distinctness conserves the individuality of God and man. "Chasms do not individuate," of course, as Josiah Royce rightly said. Yet, given individuation, do not chasms follow? God occupies a different space from man. When he is near to man, he is near as God and not as something which can in any way be confused with man.

Spatial transcendence has an important bearing on the meaning of God's omnipresence. To say that God is omnipresent does not mean simply that he is everywhere present. God ought not be thought to permeate the universe like a fog or a fragrance. Omnipresence indicates the way God is *wholly* (omni-) present wherever he is present. When God is "in" man or "in" history, he is there as himself, indivisibly. To say God is in man is to say his space is in man's space without compromising the distinctness of the space of either. The witness of the Holy Spirit of God is not a merging of God's spirit with man's but a meeting of two spirits. God does not parcel himself out. There is no composition in his being. When he is met, he is met as God and not as some diffuse extension of his being. It is truer to say with Plato that God is in man as a sailor is in a boat, or to say with Martin Buber that God is in man as air is in the lungs, than to say with immanentalists that God is in man as blood is in the veins. "You may talk as much as you like of the divine immanence," said P. T. Forsyth, "so long as you remember that it is the immanence of the transcendent." When God is in man, he is in man as God and not as man or as a fragment of God. There are no fragments of God in men, for wherever God is present he is present as himself. Man lives over against God, not "out of" or "off of" God. The proper role of man in relation to a spatially distinct God is the role of responsibility. Man and God cannot be responsibly together except as they are distinctly apart.

If God is so different from man and so distinct from him, how can man ever come into any kind of communion with God? Transcendence does not rule out communion, because it is *dimensional* as well as spatial and qualitative. Dimensional transcendence is a notion Karl Heim developed for the precise purpose of illustrating God's coordinability with a level of reality so distinct from him as human history. For dimensional transcendence is a category which retains the distinctness of spatial transcendence without limiting the meaning of transcendence to analogies drawn simply from juxtaposition. It does more justice to the Christian's sense of God's intimacy.

In a flat universe, Heim suggests, where there are only two dimensions, no more than two perpendicular lines can intersect at one point. In a universe with more than two dimensions, a universe with not only height and breadth but depth as well, an infinite number of perpendicular lines can intersect at one point. The force of this analogy for Karl Heim is twofold. First of all, on this analogy the God-dimension can be present to an infinite number of existences without jeopardy to the fullness of God's presence in each. The image intended is that somehow all of human history, notwithstanding its spatial and chronological extension and its personal individuation can participate fully in the presence of God. The God dimension is the eschatological history that intersects our world history, everywhere repairing our fragmentation by the presence of God in his wholeness.

The second use of the dimensional analogy is to say that when these lines meet they are not mutually exclusive. The intersection can be intimate and all-embracing, with genuine coordination and over-lap, without jeopardizing the distinctiveness and discreteness of each. God's presence, being dimensionally transcendent, can permeate the life of man without compromising the self-identity of either God or man.

Each of these types of transcendence performs an excellent service in clarifying the character of God's presence. The most definitive aspect of God's transcendence, however, is what might be called *functional*. For this characteristic contributes to the others their content and rationale. As has been said, God is different from man and distinct from man by what he is. Notwithstanding these cleavages, God is transcendent in such a way that man can enter into fellowship with him. Beneath all this, however, one can also say that God is present to man in such a way as to enforce a structure in which God remains irrevocably God, the possible one, the power of man's being. God is man's beginning and his end, his source and his destiny, his past and his future, the possibility of man. That is his function as God, a function no one but God is either called or equipped to perform.

This notion has the value of underplaying the purely spatial metaphors with their connotation of distance and remoteness without at the same time dissolving the structural connotations. The boundary or frontier or limit in the relation between God and man is like the boundary that defines the limit between super-sonic speed and the speed of sound. One knows he is up against it not by objective marks at the frontier but by the tremor in his being. Like the boundary which marks off the stratosphere, he knows he is about to transgress it by the sense of suffocation in his spirit. God is and does what man can never be and do. Hence, man ought never live under the conditions of history without trans-parent acknowledgement of this irreversible relation. Its folly would parallel that of the Lapland travellers Melville writes about who refused to wear colored glasses because they could not believe all the colors of the spectrum were hidden in the whiteness of the snow. They went blind.

II. THE BOUNDARY OF GOD'S NEARNESS

Logic classifies relations of functional transcendence as asymmetric. In all possible dyadic relations, it is the most definitive form of predication. From the Christian standpoint, it is also the most definitive way to characterize God's relation to history.

One might simply say, for instance, that God's presence means his nearness. That could satisfy piety, but it would not satisfy accuracy. For the relation of nearness is what is called a symmetrical relation. The perpendicular lines Karl Heim talks about in his analogy from dimensions are symmetrically related. That is to say, if line A is perpendicular to line B, line B is necessarily perpendicular to line A. It is not true to say, however, that if God is near to man, man is necessarily near to God. The God-man relation is not a symmetrical relation.

Or, one might simply say that God loves man. That would be a true statement in the context of Christian faith. But it could be misleading. It is less misleading than to say God is near man, for it adds specificity to the vaguer notion of nearness. To proximity is added the connotation of affection. But it is more accurate for another reason. It is a non-symmetrical relation. In symmetrical relations, what one says of the relation of A to B necessarily pertains to the relation of B to A, such as nearness, or the meeting of perpendicular lines. In non-symmetrical relations, what you say of the relation of A to B does not necessarily pertain to the relation of B to A. Just because God loves man does not necessarily mean that man loves God. Love is a non-symmetrical reference, hence more precise than any symmetrical relation can be. Basically, however, the God-man relation is not non-symmetrical.

To refer to God as man's author and finisher, his beginning and his end, his possibility, is to employ the most decisive structuring in the language about God's relation to man. It is a structure which dominates and defines all other references to the relation. For "the possibility of" is an asymmetrical reference and denotes a relation which is strictly irreversible. What pertains to the relation of God to man necessarily does not pertain to the relation of man to God. The God whose vocation it is to hold man by his creative hand can never be manipulated by man. The God who is co-ordinable with man nevertheless meets man within the terms of reality as structured by the asymmetry in this relation. When God is near to man, man is near to God in the asymmetry of an ir-reversible, transcendent relation. When God is near to man in love, that love is an invocation to response and not a necessary characteristic of reality. God's love is the love of a Creator for a creature, and not an instance of easy reciprocity.

The poet Hölderlin has captured this structure in the opening lines of his poem, *Patmos.*

> Near is
> The God, and hard to grasp.

Here the vague symmetrical reference, "nearness," is structured by the more precise asymmetry, "hard to grasp."

Instances abound in the language of piety. The pious have not always realized, however, how disciplined the language is and how calculated to conserve authenticity between God and history. "How far removed art thou from my vision, though I am so near to thine." Anselm wrote that in his *Proslogium.* (16) Augustine achieves a similar clarity when extolling the Light which is God: "Nor was it above my soul as oil is above water nor yet as heaven above earth: but higher than my soul because it made me; and I below it, because I was made by it."[1]

To say that God is present is to say that he is neither beyond history nor within history. He is the limit of history, the boundary, the frontier, the possibility of history. Existential history experi-ences this limit as God's absence. Eschatological history experiences

[1] *Confessions* X, 27, 38.

it as God's presence, the very possibility of history. Existential history is the story of how man bruises himself in the world in his oversight of the structure of reality. Eschatological history is the story of how man experiences God transparently as the inescapable condition under which all life is lived.

Wherever a man may flee, God is there. This is so not because man carries God around in himself, and not because God is just indiscriminately everywhere, but because human history is set within theistic conditions, conditions which make God the primal presupposition of all reality. The freedom of man's possibility to roam the distances between heaven and hell is the freedom existential history transcribes. That freedom never really actualizes its possibility, however. It remains in the falsehood of penultimacy until it is transcended through the realization of the prior freedom of God to be man's possibility. Man's freedom is a freedom toward nothing until it is set within the structure in which God is free to be God. "Even truer than our freedom and truer than the wretched truth of our *servum arbitrium,* is the heartening truth that God is free."[2]

Man is free to know God. That freedom is in vain, however, until it is transcended by God's freedom to be present. That means that the knowledge of God cannot be sought on the same conditions under which the knowledge of world historical existence is sought. The God who is present as the hidden possibility of existence and of our knowledge of existence cannot be drawn into the sphere of customary knowledge. He must be allowed to remain God even in the moment in which he would be known. As the possibility of the knowledge of everything else, God is known in a different way from everything else. He cannot therefore be enfolded into man's perceptual or conceptual experience as one existence alongside of others. He is not at the beck and call of

---

[2] Karl Barth, *Die Kirchliche Dogmatik,* III/2, p. 43. Cf. Robert Osborn, *The Idea of Freedom in the Theology of Karl Barth,* unpublished doctoral dissertation, Drew University, Madison, N. J., 1955.

man's acquisitive intellect. He is destined to be present to the
knowledge of man as the hidden, the possible, the transcendent
one. All man's knowledge of God will reflect the structure in God's
way of being present. For a Christian to say, "I know God," is
therefore to engage in equivocation; for he does not "know" God
as he knows in general. The Christian knowledge of God is the
knowledge that God knows us, holds all our knowledge under the
evaluation of his own prior and objective being, calls us by name,
numbers the hairs on our head, watches our fall as he watches the
sparrow's.

Man is free to do God's will. That freedom is in vain, however,
unless man realizes that God is a God who swears by nothing other
than himself. Man's freedom to do God's will is set within the
conditions of God's freedom to will. God is ethically free just as
he is epistemologically free, for he is the source and possibility of
the law just as he is the source and possibility of knowledge. He
knows no good but what he wills. The ethical life in the presence
of God, therefore, is the life that holds itself responsible to the
evaluating judgment of God. It is the life that refuses to bind God
to the level of man's moral insight or even to the history of God's
own judgments. It resolves to keep man's sentiment for virtue
under suspension to God's morally free and creative presence.
Kierkegaard's concept of "the teleological suspension of the ethical"
is a document in eschatological history, for it expressed the understanding that God is the beginning and the end of morality. The
judgments of the world ought never therefore be allowed to re-
verse the structure that says God is always first. They must remain
porous and permeable to the free decisions of God in his relation
to the process of history.

Man is free to live in God's world. That freedom is in vain,
however, unless man realizes that the cosmos comes alive only
when God speaks. That is the source of everything discernible as
its order, just as it is the source of everything discernible as its
novelty. Laws of nature are as tentative as laws of ethics, and for

the same reason. God is prior to both. That is his freedom as the possible one. God is not bound to his universe, or to the statistical averages in the probabilities which the natural sciences observe. If the daily rising of the sun takes on the character of predictable regularity, one ought not think that it could do no other. One ought rather to realize that "every morning God says to the sun, 'Get up'," as G. K. Chesterton was fond of observing. It must not be thought, however, that the knowledge of God's freedom toward the world is a kind of knowledge about the natural world. It is rather interpretation by which a Christian may learn to live in the world by letting God be its Lord.

Man is free to move through history. His freedom is in vain, however, unless he acknowledges that "the way of man is not in himself."[3] The story of man's past is not an adequate basis for negotiating his life in the future. For God is not tied to man's past. If one does not know this, he misses the very important difference between Herodotus and Isaiah. The Greek historians transcribed the past for the regularities in history by which to plan the future. The Hebrew historians were mainly prophets who implored their people to keep the future open to the influences of the living God. Any historian knows that the orderly and rational picture of human history dug from the chronicle of past events is staggered by the ambiguities in man's emerging present. But man lives neither by his past nor by his present, but by God's hidden presence. Man lives by what God is doing, and the deeds of God are always to man a future, a living largely in hope because established upon a God who is making history. To be sure, God in the past has made covenants with his people which are binding upon the future. But these covenants are of a structural sort designed to commit man to allowing God to be the Lord of the future. Prophetic recollection of the covenants of past history are ways of reminding the people of who God is, a God who has promised to be the Lord of the future. Man must therefore let God be Lord.

[3] Jeremiah 10:23.

The freedoms of man need not be in vain, for God's presence is not in vain. Hölderlin, who knew how hard God is to grasp, also knew that the transcendent God who lives in freedom is a God whose presence is very near.

> That which thou seekest
> Is near, and already coming to meet thee.
> —(*Homecoming*)

In the Old Testament, God's presence is believed to be the appearance not of God, but of his "glory." "Glory of God" signified any moment in history in which God was not present in vain. At a decisive moment in Israel's history, however, "the glory of God" became a synonym of Israel's hope projected upon the future. When Jesus appeared as the Christ, he was proclaimed to be "the Lord of glory."[4] The title has a twofold significance for Christians. First of all, Christ is himself regarded as the presence of God in glory. That is to say that in view of Christ God is not present in vain. Second, the history which lives from the glory of God's presence in Christ is the eschatological history, and the people who adopt Christ as the Lord of glory and allow his appearance to form their existence, is the eschatological community, the Church. A Christian is one who is swept up out of the existential lack in world history into the eschatological community where history is not in vain because it is life *in via* "from glory to glory."[5] Christ is the presence of God and his presence gives history its ultimate end, therefore its hope of being history.

III. LOVE CROSSES THE BOUNDARY

The historical presence of God is achieved in Christ. There the limit of being which separates God and man is overcome. That is the great "new mystery" about which the early fathers knew. The structure which says God is God and man is man has been upended at one point, and that from God's side. When the tran-

[4] I Cor. 2:8; James 2:1.
[5] 2 Cor. 3:7 ff.

scendent God crosses into history in Christ, he does not abrogate the structure. He illustrates it.

John Calvin has said that God was on earth without leaving heaven. That is in one sense a piece of first century mythology. In another sense it is a highly figurative way of elucidating the dialectical tension in the life of God. There are no other instances in which the faithfulness of God is achieved by a device so traumatic ontologically. Christ is God's cardinal redemptive act. It is not the fact that there are no comparable cases, however, that makes this event unique. It is unique because there can be no other instance. Christ is the historical presence of the fulness of God. He is the *totus intra carnem*. The early creeds of the church meant to affirm this seriousness of God with history when they located the Son of God wholly on the Creator side of the Creator-creature structure without ceasing to refer to God as one, and without ceasing to refer to Jesus of Nazareth as the Son of God. The meaning of Christ as Son of God is the historical presence of the hidden God.

It is not being claimed that when the hidden God is present he ceases to be hidden. That would be tantamount to saying God can cease to be God. To say that the hidden God reveals himself in Christ as present is to say he reveals himself there. As Luther says, God at the breast of Mary? God at a carpenter's bench? God on a cross? Who would think to look for him there? For Christians to act as if God's revelation is in history as other historical phenomena are there makes of Christianity a form of paganism where existing objects become objects of worship. The revelation is not world history; it is eschatological history. It is not the object of our possible knowledge, but the event which makes our knowledge possible. It is not a datum of science, but an act of the historical reason, originating in the interplay of two spiritual freedoms, God's and man's. It is not in history, except in the very specialized sense of the boundary of history—where one history ends and the other begins. It is the hinge of history. By his hiddenness even in revelation God escapes the irony of the debutante who "comes out" as an attractive object in order to win a lover and finds herself being loved for life as an object.

A Christian is one who is inexplicably moved to choose the event of Christ as the presence of God and to make that event the very form of his existence, the beginning of his new life. Appropriation of God's revelation as saving knowledge is as asymmetric as the God-relation itself: it is a possibility in God's action in history and not in ours. Hugh of St. Victor has stated the case with tender simplicity. "He comes hidden, unseen, and imperceptible. He comes to touch you, not to be seen by you; to admonish you, not to be beheld. He comes not to give Himself entirely, but to present Himself to your awareness."[1]

The meaning of the presence of the hidden God is that God's presence be not in vain but rather a presence *pro nobis*. The post-Christian Gnostics saw this as clearly and dramatically as anyone. History, they found, was proceeding in culpable disregard of the boundary between God and man. Man in history was battering that boundary in the futile effort to rise to heights belonging to God alone. That ill-conceived siege against the wall of heaven produced in the ontologically insensitive the psychologically alarming moods of melancholy and dread, of fear and anxiety, clear symptoms that man was somehow living against his vocation. The evident parallels between Gnosticism's description of the human predicament and what one finds in existential philosophies and psychoanalytic case studies is most impressive.

The Son of God, the Gnostics believed, was sent across the ontological boundary between God and history to reveal to man what it means to be a man and to induce history to acknowledge the boundaries which the structure of reality imposes upon human life. In abysmal irresponsibility toward the structure in reality which says that God as the limit of history cannot come out of hiding,

[1] *Soliloquy on the Earnest Money of the Soul*, Marquette University Press, 1956, p. 35.

mankind was writing a history of wretchedness in its effort to bring divinity to birth. The Gnostics believed the Son of God was sent across the boundary between invisibility and visibility to instruct mankind in what is and what is not accessible to historical knowledge. They did not believe—as is often mistakenly thought about such Gnostics as the Valentinians—that the Son of God came to teach the infinite details about God, as if information about God were in itself redemptive. The Son of God was sent to communicate the one bit of redemptive news, that God is not a God who can be held at the end of the human reach. As Irenaeus said somewhat sympathetically about the Gnostic doctrine, when the understanding becomes satisfied that God is unknowable, it is restored to health.[2] The truth of the Gnostic scheme is that Christology is soteriology. That means that God turned to history in Christ in order that man might have a history on ontologically authentic terms.

The "new mystery" (Melito of Sardis) of the Christian faith is not that God is real, but that he is present and that his presence is not in vain. God hurts himself in the act of overcoming the structure that separates him from man. In the act he dramatizes the existence of the structure. In that act God loves the world. He loves the world in such a way as to evoke man's responsive, affectionate assumption of the human role.

In the Christian faith, what is decisive for man about God is not God's being, but his presence. In the light of what God *is*, God is man's tempter. He is an object of competition, stirring up the marathon runner in man's soul and leading him to overreach himself. Man is a being who will not easily concede a race. He will not be superseded. God is the being who, by virtue of his exclusive prerogative as God, becomes the occasion for the deepest temptation in the human spirit. In the light of who God *is*, he is primarily a jealous God who will not tolerate any oversight by man. Jealousy in God, as the *Epistle of James* makes clear, is appropriate

[2] *Against Heresies*, II, xviii, 2.

to God chiefly because it is so inappropriate to man. Only God has the right to be first, and God has the responsibility of vigilance over the line between himself and history. When man reflects the existence of realities other than God to the exclusion of the reality of God, God has no alternative but jealousy. Schleiermacher was wrong to refuse to attribute characteristics to God which one would find revolting in one's friends. Jealousy is incompatible with human life in the same way God-almightyness is. That is, it is appropriate only to God.

The decisive thing about God for the Christian faith is the way he uses his transcendent freedom to avert man's using his freedom in vain. God who is free to be God uses his freedom to become present in human history in the event of Christ. Hereafter, it is not religiously edifying to attempt to understand God without the mediation of Jesus Christ. To see God in his being is to see the qualities which evoke the temptation not to trust him and hence to feel the rage of his jealous spirit. Nothing is more conducive to asperity in man than aseity in God. Seen in Christ, however, God is not simply *a se*, resplendent in his transcendent singularity. He is *pro nobis*, sacrificing himself across the limit of history to make his presence known in Christ, for us. To understand God in Christ is to see that God is a God who hurts himself upon the very boundary against which man is hurting himself, in order to reconcile man to his vocation as a man. He is a God who loves, whose suffering is a seal of his love, and whose suffering love provides the possibility of man's response of love. "This is the greatest proof of the goodness of God," said Clement of Alexandria. "Estranged by nature, yet he cares for us."[3] As the Bible says, we love him because he first loved us. His act of love makes man's love possible.

Apart from this act by which God incarnates himself in human history to reconcile man, it is ambiguous to say that God is good, or love, or faithful. God is *God*. All predication beyond that ir-

[3] *Miscellanies* II, xvi.

reversible ontological structure takes on the aspect of a subjective valuing of God. To say that God *is* love and mean by that an attribute or a perfection or the very essence of God courts real peril. It is the peril of evaluating God by identifying his being with love, thus inverting the very structure at the ground of his deity. It is rather out of his freedom to be God that he loves. His love is an act in history. The act has the effect of invoking man's sensitive response to the ontological topography which is the limit of man's being.

To say that God *is* love is to create an ontology out of the unreflective witness of Christian piety. If "God *is* love," then "God *must* love." That identifies love with God's nature. But in Jesus Christ the love of God is history, and not nature. The ontological presupposition of God's *act* of love in Christ is not the nature of love in God, but his freedom to be God. Love born of nature is necessary, and therefore less than love. Love in history is free. One ought not to infer from God's reconciling act in Christ to a "redemptive principle" in God, as it is so popular to do in theology today. Process theology makes this mistake in its most deceptive form when it describes a structure in reality in which God need not incarnate himself in history because all history is necessarily "incarnational" in its meaning. Mercy in that view is not an option for God.

There is really only one thing God must be. He must be God. But that is enough. That knowledge unacknowledged tempts all history against its true vocation. God does not leave history in its ignorance, however. In the freedom of his transcendent being he plunges across the ontological barrier, stretches himself from heaven to earth in the life-time of Jesus of Nazareth, to bring to man the good news that He, the father of Jesus, alone is God. In that act, He loves the world in a way that reconciles the world to life in history and to his lordship over history. By that act the old age of the absence of God, where nothing is finally possible, has passed away. The new age, the ultimate age of possibility in God's presence has come.

CHAPTER

7

THE HISTORICITY OF CHRIST

THE Christian faith has its source in an event. Jesus Christ *happened* in the midst of a people. He came as the very *act* of God. His appearance set off a chain of *events*, the church. His presence, therefore, is a hinge. Happening in time, he both connects and separates the old and the new, the past and the future. Von Hügel was right, therefore, to refer to the "sheer happenedness" in Christianity.

One of the large claims in this volume, however, is that there is no adequate consensus today as to what history is or as to whether there can really be a history in any finally meaningful sense. It has been my thesis that the understanding of history implicit in the Christian faith can end that ambiguity. Yet, judgment must begin with the household of God. If Christ as the presence of God is the end of history, the very meaning of history is under suspension until clarification is forthcoming regarding what it means that Christ is historical. As long as Christ is not unambiguously historical, there can be no consensus as to what history is and whether history is therefore finally possible.

I. TRUTH WHICH HAPPENS

Confusion about the meaning of history dates as far back as the beginning of the Christian movement. The truth of God entered human events in Jesus Christ, but as I have already indicated, the

169

available categories for expressing this event came from the Greeks who had little interest in events. Actually, they had a positive aversion to anything that "happened." Ultimate truth for Greek philosophy does not happen; it simply is. Events were self-incriminating. Their very "happenedness" was a sign they were transitory and lacked finality.

The Christians testified that the presence of God "happened" in Jesus Christ. Yet when they gave systematic expression to that witness, they allowed Christ's temporal eventfulness to be overshadowed by his eternal and unchanging being. The intellectual agonies of the early creeds reveal an uncongenial alliance between Greek and Christian categories. An instance of this is the Chalcedonian creed with its substantialistic parallelism of true godhood and true manhood in Jesus Christ, which "suppresses one of the dimensions of the gospel Kerygma, time."[1]

Today the historicity of the faith is prominent in the concern of every theologian. The old decision between Greek categories and Hebrew categories has lost much of its cruciality. To say that the Greeks affirm eternal truths of reason while the Hebrews affirm the truth of events is now virtually a theological banality. Theologians are almost unanimous that Christian truth is something which happens.

Another Greek endowment of theology affects the Christian understanding of history at a different point, however. Affiliated as are events and time, an influential bequest of Greece to the Christian theology of history was its view of time. Time, which Plato called the moving image of eternity, is always slipping into the past. Events, which happen in time, must always be considered like nature from an objective and spatial distance. Thereafter, when the Christian faith was written in the Platonic tradition, what was meant by its historicity was that it is somehow tied up with the irrevocable but irrecoverable facts of the past. Likewise, time,

[1] J. L. Leuba, L'Institution et L'événement, quoted in Jean Daniélou, Essai sur le Mystère de l'Histoire, Paris, Editions du Seuil, 1953, p. 162.

which Aristotle called a measurable succession of moments, can be stretched out like a panorama, like the spectacle of nature. It can be measured by numbered spaces on a map or the sweep of the clock's hand. Thereafter, when one said in the Aristotelian tradition that Christianity is historical, he meant that he could map out the dispensations of God's grace and chart the time-table in God's plan of salvation. Jesus Christ, happening on the landscape of time, becomes by this view an object for cartographer and chronologist alike.

Augustine had more of a sense for history than any theologian before him, except possibly Irenaeus. But Augustine found the historical character of Christianity baffling in the context of this Greek heritage. Was he not tempted toward the common-sense view of time which Greek philosophy had standardized, when he said, "What now is clear and plain is, that neither things to come nor past are"?[2] If history is the factuality of past events stretching out seriatim, and what is past is not; and if Christ is said to be historical, how can he who is past be our Lord in the present?

In the context of this kind of question it does not seem strange that theologians should have denied Christ is historical. For by that denial they intended to affirm the reality of Christ as present. It does not seem strange that Franz Overbeck, the Basel church historian of the last century, would insist that "if it is Christianity, then it is not history. If it is history, then it is not Christianity."[3] Nor was it strange that the Zürich pastor, Hermann Kutter, would pronounce that Christ is our present, immediate Lord, and "the immediate has no history,"[4] or that Ernst Troeltsch, the German theologian, would declare, "History is no place for absolute per-

---

[2] Confessions XI, 26.
[3] Karl Barth's paraphrase of Overbeck's position in a review of Overbeck's Christentum und Kultur entitled "Unerledigte Anfragen an die heutige Theologie," in Zur inneren Lage des Christentums, Munich, Kaiser, 1920; p. 9.
[4] Das Unmittelbare, Basel, Kober C.F. Spittlers Nachfolger, 1921, p. 321.

sons or absolute religions; history and absolute are contradictory."[5] Actually, there is very little self-evident history in the writings of Paul the apostle. That is to say, Paul speaks not of what is past, but of the presence of the living Lord, not of world history, but of freedom from the world in its old form. It is the presence of Christ and not his past which confers upon Paul the same apostolic status given the original disciples. And the contemporary Christian claims continuity with Paul because of the Christian's own relation to Christ. For Jesus Christ is not the "I was" but the "I am." To contemplate him is not to stand away from him at an historical distance but to enter into his life now.

Contemporary theology inherits both the sense of the historicity of the Christian faith and the protests against its historicity.[6] The traditional churches have conserved the sense of history, arching over time to hinge the present to the past. The sectarian groups and mystics have conserved the protest against history by their flight beyond successiveness and their intimate perpendicular communion with the being of God. The current great assumption in Christian theology is that the Christian faith has to do with the historical. The question remains, however, as to whether this truth can be expressed without either falling into archaism or reacting from archaism into docetism. Can we now take the historical character of the Christian faith seriously without making theology a branch of the historical sciences, always striving to recover an irrecoverable past—a labor of Sisyphus? Or can we resist the temptation to abandon the potentially sterile tasks of the historian and install theology as the handmaiden of a kind of non-historical mysticism? These extremes can be outflanked if the common-sense view of history, dignified and authorized for western thought by

[5] *Die Absolutheit des Christentums*, third edition. Tübingen, J.C.B. Mohr, 1912, p. 33.
[6] For a most sensitive discussion of this subject by an American theologian, see Albert C. Outler, *The Christian Tradition and the Unity We Seek*, Oxford, 1957.

Greek philosophy, is amended by the dimension of meaning implicit in history as eschatological.

II. THE HINGE BETWEEN THE TIMES

Jesus Christ is "the hinge of history." I have drawn the metaphor not from Winston Churchill but from the French Catholic theologian, Jean Daniélou.[1] However, I do not use the metaphor as Daniélou does. Daniélou follows Oscar Cullmann in the service of a linear view of time. I do not mean, as they do, that Christ hinges together some past time, even the times of the history of Israel, with the Christian future. That would be to reimport the Greek and common-sense view of time. Rather, I mean that Christ takes all times off their hinges and becomes himself the Lord of time. (I Timothy 1:17) As Lord of time he holds all moments together in the coinherence of his life. (Colossians 1:17) To know who he is means to have a history. For history is life with a meaning, and only one who is at the beginning and at the end of time, only one who is the Lord of time holds all times together. Only he who is the fulness of time fills time with the ultimate meaning that constitutes it as history.

Hegel sensed this truth, though dimly, when he affirmed that to live with meaning each man must in his own short life relive the whole journey of mankind. What was a protean project for Hegel is a divine gift for the simplest Christian. Irenaeus made that truth patent when he pictured Christ as the man who perfectly recapitulates the life of every other man and on his behalf. Albert Camus, the French existentialist, is even more radical about the requirements for meaningful life. "History only exists in the final analysis to God,"[2] he claims, for only God begins and ends the whole gamut of man's times. But what is true for God is given in Christ, the Lord of time. To be with Christ is to have the presence of God, the beginning and the end of all things. Even to live

[1] Op. cit., p. 193.
[2] The Rebel, Knopf, 1953, p. 256.

in the Old Testament is to live in pre-history, for the Old Testament lives toward the end from the beginning. But to be in the New Testament, in the faith in Christ is to live from the beginning *and* the end, hence to have history. A Christian lives in history, not because he undergoes a process of time—not even because he undergoes a process for which he is able, by imagination and speculation, to provide an orderly pattern of explanation. He lives in history because he is confronted by Jesus Christ who is the beginning and the end, and thus confers upon each moment of the process the whole meaning of the process.

Without the fulness of time, without the fulfilled event of Christ, our lives fall forward ambiguously. With it they are supported by a completed purpose. Without the fulness of time we live toward a diffuse and ill-defined future. With it we know that God is our future. This happening transforms "sheer happenedness" into history. "From this moment onwards," as the Gospels put it, (Matthew 26:64; Luke 22:69) our past becomes pre-history, our future is filled with purpose, and our present already lives by a fulfilled hope. (Ephesians 1:14)

This structure of past, present, and future is no longer the chronological sequence of measured time. It is the transition from the abyss in our wake, which is nihilism or death, to the luminous immensity ahead, which is salvation or life. Past, present, and future as successive moments are telescoped into one redemptive moment in the presence of the "I am" for whom past, present and future are one. (Hebrews 13:8; Revelation 1:8, 22:13) Now "we have been born anew to a living hope through the resurrection of Jesus Christ from the dead." (I Peter 1:3) God has overlooked the "times of our ignorance" when it was not known that Christ was the Lord of time and the fulness of time. (Acts 17:30-31) Christ is the beginning and the end of all things, and he is now "at hand." (I Peter 4:7; cf. Mark 1, Galatians 4, Ephesians 1)

After the appearance of Christ in the time of man, the whole concept of linear successiveness is set askew. Christ walks up and down the pages of world history with very little consideration for its consecutive character, much as a fly walks back and forth across the calendar on the wall. In so doing, a dimension beyond chronological time is insinuated. Moses is said to speak of Christ, Abraham to be saved by his faith in Christ, and the thief on the cross will be with Christ in paradise three days in advance of Christ's own resurrection. This contradiction of our customary prejudice about the irreversibility of chronological time has modern science as its ally—as in the case of Miss Bright of limerick fame:

> There was a young girl named Miss Bright,
> Who could travel much faster than light.
> She departed one day,
> In an Einsteinian way,
> And came back on the previous night.[3]

It is curious that some theologians are willing to demythologize the space concepts of the Bible but not the time concepts.[4] What they usually guard in the concept of time, however, is precisely its spatial character, that is, its chronological successiveness. Are not such words as "past" and "future" fully as symbolic as the words "above" and "below," and do they not in most instances carry spatial connotations, as Aristotle long ago pointed out, illustrated in the words "before" and "after?"[5] It is clear that the common-sense view of history is prominent in the Bible. It could not be otherwise. Our "natural" outlook on things dictates it. But in the "Biblical" outlook, the distinctive and decisive emphasis is not the common-sense view. Faith affirms not so much that Jesus

[3] Quoted in George Gamow's *One Two Three . . . Infinity*, Mentor, 1953, p. 105.
[4] Théo Preiss, *La Vie en Christ*, chapter translated in English under the title "The Vision of History in the New Testament," *Journal of Religion*, XXX, No. 3, July, 1950, p. 168.
[5] *Physics* 219a. I am indebted to the work of the Japanese theologian, Seiichi Hatano, for calling attention to this passage. See his *Time and Eternity* (*Toki to eien*), *Collected Works*, Vol. V., Tokyo, 1949.

Christ is in history as that Jesus Christ constitutes history. "Revelation is not a predicate of history but history is a predicate of revelation."[6] Quite obviously Jesus Christ is a happening in the time of the world. That knowledge, however, is not the good news of the Christian faith. The gospel is that Jesus Christ has unhinged our worldly times and refastened them to the life of God.

I became certain of the soundness of my son's theological instincts the evening I asked him if he knew what time it was, and he replied with a question.

"No; what time *is* it?"

I said, "It's 8:30!"

Whereupon he replied with what Samuel Beckett has called "a fine Dostoievskian contempt for the vulgarity of a plausible concatenation,"[7] "What does *that* mean?"

Time tells us nothing we can live by. Time gets its importance from the events it measures. The meaning of eight-thirty is "bedtime." There is likewise a time for marrying. The time does not qualify the marriage; marriage qualifies the time. There is a time for dying. It is not that death gets its meaning from the time of its occurrence. Death occurring endows the moment with its meaning. Nor is the presence of God in Christ a quality of time; it rather qualifies time, as salt qualifies one dish and not another. The distinction lies not in the food but in the presence of the salt.[8]

Gerhard Krüger, a contemporary German philosopher, in his influential lecture entitled *History in the Thought of the Present* has given philosophical expression to the ingredients in this view of history.

> Every solution of the problem of history presupposes that history be essentially at an end; it can indeed reckon with

[6] Karl Barth, *Die Kirchliche Dogmatik* I, 2, Zurich, 1945, p. 64.
[7] *Proust*, Evergreen, p. 62.
[8] An illustration used by Friedrich Gogarten in *Ich glaube an den dreieinigen Gott*, Jena, 1927, p. 111. Cf. Thorleif Boman's study, *Das Hebräische Denken im Vergleich mit dem Griechischen*, Göttingen, 1954, especially pp. 104-133, "Zeit und Raum."

an open future but only so that the truth already discovered
in principle must still be brought to universal preeminence.
. . . The possibility of understanding history from within
history rests simply on this, that history has already become
essentially comprehensible as a whole.[9]

Nowhere in the entire delineation of the events which constitute
our falling forward can we point and say, "There is the end," except in Jesus Christ. To treat the event of Christ biographically
and thus to make of Christ a participant in our history is, of course,
a possibility in his very manner of appearing. But that would be
a secularization of the gospel, for the gospel says he is among us
as the exalted source of our meaningful life.

Secular counterparts of this eschatological view of history are
instructive. Marxism illustrates it, dividing time as it does into
pre-history and history, with history beginning at the proletarian
revolt. The intention of time which constitutes history of our
process is not present, according to Marx, before that moment.
Nehru addressed the people of India in a similar manner on the
occasion of their liberation: "The appointed day has come. The
turning point is past. History begins anew for us." The French
Imperialists illustrate this secularization of Christian eschatology
when they say, "Without North Africa . . . France would have
no history in the 21st century."[10] By this they do not mean that
France would cease to exist, to move eventfully through linear
time. They simply mean that the existence of France would be
unsupportable with the loss of her colony. A persuasive illustration
can be adduced from the sort of experience D. H. Lawrence
sketches. Separated from his beloved Lady Cynthia, he writes to
her, "We have no history, since we saw you last. I feel as if I had
less than no history—as if I had spent those five months in a

[9] *Die Geschichte im Denken der Gegenwart,* Frankfurt, Wissenschaft und
Gegenwart, No. 16, 1947, p. 24.
[10] *Time* Magazine, September 5, 1955, p. 12.

tomb."[11] To be isolated from the be-all and end-all of one's existence is to be more dead than alive.

The confession that Jesus Christ creates our history is the
acknowledgment that he is the source of our meaningful life. We
cannot then discuss him without presupposing him. When you
presuppose him, you have entered into the history which he
creates. It is therefore unprofitable if not unintelligible to insist,
as various theologians do, geared to a common-sense view of time,
that the revelational events recorded in the Bible "took place at
a certain historical time and place"; or that the covenant relationship with God in the Bible "is a matter of historical fact"; or that
Christianity is an historical religion because it "presents us with
religious doctrines which are at the same time historical events."[12]
The historical character of the Christian faith inheres in the way in
which the exalted Christ constitutes our history. We have not the
historical Jesus but the exalted Christ to worship. Nor have we
Abraham and Moses to remember, but Christ. He is near us in a
way in which no other past is present. Abraham and Moses are
in our religious memory, but not as Christ is. While we may re-
enact from the past the days both of Moses and of Christ, the
Christ remembered is infinitely closer to us than the Moses remembered. For Christ's nearness is not an attribute of his relative
temporal proximity. He is near because he constitutes our history,
as, for instance, Moses does not. Origen has rightly said of the
event of Christ, "The shadow-Jerusalem then lost what substance
it had,"[13] as do all pre-enactments of the fulness of time. For on
Christ, an event in our time, all our history hinges.

I would even propose that it is unintelligible to refer to the

[11] The Portable D.H. Lawrence, N.Y., Viking, 1955; p. 569. Letter written
January 30, 1915.
[12] G. Ernest Wright, God Who Acts, Regnery, 1952, p. 50; Alan Richardson,
Christian Apologetics, Harpers 1947, p. 91; Herbert Butterfield, Christianity
and History, Scribners, 1950, p. 3.
[13] Quoted in Jean Daniélou, Origen, tr. by Walter Mitchell, Sheed and Ward,
1955, p. 154.

resurrection of Jesus Christ from the dead as an historical fact. Thomas Arnold, Oxford history professor and Rugby headmaster, called the resurrection "the best-attested fact in history" but with that so-called "fact" he was impotent to save Matthew Arnold from skepticism. For the reality of the resurrection is not its factuality, not that it happened in the past, but that it happens in our present and saves our past from death by tying our future to the living Christ, and thus redeeming our time.

It would not be at all perverse if one were to ask at this juncture, "Nevertheless, did it not happen?" For there is a "sheer happenedness" in the Christian revelation, and the Easter event is its apex. But, with the raising of that question one ought not assume everyone knows what is meant by a "happening."[14] And if one were to insist that we locate the resurrection of Christ somewhere in the chronological series which characterizes man's time, I would not deny that it can be done; I would simply deny that it can be done profitably. For the announcement of the resurrection of Christ is not meant to add to our knowledge of world history but to take the hinges off that very knowledge and give our life a history in him.

III. THE NEW "QUEST OF THE HISTORICAL JESUS"

The concern with existential and eschatological dimensions of history is not meant to be a denial of world history and Biblical history. Nor is there even the suspicion here that existential and eschatological history deal with the meanings of events, while world history and Biblical history are preoccupied only with their

---

14 Cf. The altercation between Barth and Bultmann on the resurrection. Barth says the resurrection is not history, and so does Bultmann. But when Bultmann says it, Barth insists that the resurrection "happened" in a truer sense than any other happening. Vide Die kirchliche Dogmatik I, 2, p. 127; and III, 2, p. 531. On that point Bultmann asks Barth what he means by "happened." Vide Kerygma and Myth, S.P.C.K., 1953, pp. 38 ff., and "Das Problem der Hermeneutik" in Glauben und Verstehen, Vol. II, 1952, p. 234.

happenedness. World history, however, is not concerned with the final (*eschatos*) meaning of events. When it is so concerned, it becomes existential history, for world history does not advance clues to the finality of history. Biblical history, as I have been using the expression in this volume, does concern itself with the finality of history. The Old and New Testaments have that in common. In the New Testament faith, however, Jesus Christ has become the end of history, the source of the new age, the event from which history thereafter takes the form of its existence in its ultimate or eschatological sense.

Considering these meanings and distinctions, what is the bearing today of what Schweitzer long ago called the "quest of the historical Jesus"? In the last century there was a skepticism storming the church over the question as to whether Jesus ever lived. Historiographers in the tradition of Leopold von Ranke embarrassed theologians by exposing the theological inability to get to "the facts as they really happened." The church weathered the storm because it was able on the basis of scientific historiography adequately to support the claim that Jesus at least existed. In the light of what Christianity is really all about, however, that epoch in the recent history of the church has thwarted the movement of the church as sniping parties thwart the advance of panzer divisions in an all-out battle. The period had a nuisance value which has not related materially to the crucial historical objective of the faith.

The historical question at the heart of the Christian movement is not whether Jesus of Nazareth ever lived but whether there can be a history without him. It becomes a major theological burden, therefore, continually to bracket out the "quest of the historical Jesus" which is conducted in the old style, the world-historical style, in order to elevate to prominence the quest for Jesus as the presence of God and thus the source of the new age. This is not to deny the relevance of what is being done by conscientious Christian scholars devoted to documentary and archaeological research. Nor is it meant to foster again the old cleavage between the Jesus of history and the Christ of faith. The Christ of faith is the eschatological event, which is history in its fullest sense and not something beyond history. It is only to specify the several dimensions of historical responsibility and, whatever their organic relation to each other, to distinguish their separate roles.

The distinction is not unfamiliar to the methodologies we all employ in everyday life. When a person looks into the eyes of another to read his meaning, he must bracket out the question of the existence of the eye and peer into it for what is hidden there. Phenomenological philosophy calls this method "eidetic reduction." The historian brackets out the question of the object's existence in order to let its meaning appear, in the same way a portrait painter brackets out the effort at sheer photographic likeness, with all its durability and tangibility, to let the mobility of the object's soul appear.

The most historiographically sophisticated example of the quest of the historical Jesus in contemporary Biblical scholarship is found among the pupils of Bultmann. They have overridden his refusal to make the quest in the old nineteenth-century sense by making it in the new twentieth-century sense.[1] They do not search for the world-historical Jesus behind the confessional and sermonic form in which the testimony to his existence appears in the New Testament. They search for Jesus *within* that form. This is fully consistent with any historian's method who finds the data of diaries and letters more primary and illuminating historically than accounts by journalists and court clerks. Nor do they search for some object in the past which is undeniably there as any other world historical object. They simply let the data be, as sensitive historians would, and in the process Jesus emerges as the Christ, the source of meaningful existence, the eschatological event.

[1] Günther Bornkamm, Ernst Fuchs, and Ernst Käsemann; in America, James M. Robinson. *See* Robinson's article, "The Quest of the Historical Jesus Today," *Theology Today*, Vol. XV, No. 2, July, 1958.

Wherein lies the uniqueness of Christianity in such an attitude toward history? Customarily, we say Christianity is different from all faiths and philosophies in at least this one respect; its truth is bound up with historical fact. That is only partially true. There is one decided place where eternity has become time and that is the place named Jesus Christ. As Luther has said, the revelation was bound once-for-all to "a certain time, place, source, race, city, and person."[2] Kierkegaard was utterly right, therefore, to use Lessing's notion of the chance facts of history as a more adequate vehicle of Christian expression than Hegel's eternal truths of reason. And Pascal was right to class Christianity with such chance facts of history as Cleopatra's nose. Had there been no Christ in Bethlehem or on Calvary, the whole course of history would have been different. But it would be disastrous to the Christian understanding for one to pin the uniqueness of Christianity to its sheer factuality, if by that one meant its occurrence in the time of the world. For the uniqueness of the Christian faith is attached to the action of God in making Christ the author of the new age. The uniqueness of Christianity is resident not in the fact that someone called Christ once happened, but that this event is the special order of event which does not *cease* to happen. Christianity is unique because when it happens, it takes the hinges off the world, putting an end to the world and giving the world a new and different beginning.

Can one experience the "sheer happenedness" of faith without a prior knowledge of some historical facts? One cannot. This is why Israel and the church alike date the events which evoke faith and why they recite these events as the occasions for evoking faith. Again, as Luther has said, "Before faith can be expected, it is necessary that a knowledge of history occur." "This bare recital of history is the primary task of the evangelist."[3] Nothing in Christianity,

[2] *Weimar Ausgabe* 20; 219, 20-27.
[3] *Weimar Ausgabe* 32; 122, 12-15; and 27; 28, 6-8.

then, could condone an historical ignorance which would confuse the renaissance historian Campanella with major league baseball. And Dead Sea scrolls can help Christ live for us. It is important to the Bible that Isaiah saw the Lord in the year Uzziah died, and that it was under Pontius Pilate Jesus died. The significance of dated time is utterly canonical.

This emphasis can be overdone, of course. When Luke, for instance, dates the advent of Christ, he does so with reference to specifically gentile events just as Matthew does so with reference to specifically Jewish events. Their concern is not that Christ is a chronologically datable event but that he is Lord of Greek history and of Jewish history. The value of this method of dating events, that is, does not inhere in the date. As Henri de Lubac says, "The reality of history is the necessary guarantee of the mysterious reality which it signifies. . . . Neither by banal meditation nor by impersonal science does the gospel entirely free its secret."[4] Truth does not inhere in the date in world history; the date simply conserves the witness to the truth. That is to say, the dated past is important. But there is no knowledge of the word of God simply from dated time. Flesh and blood did not reveal the messianic meaning of Jesus to Peter and dated facts will not reveal the living Christ to the contemporary church. God must be allowed to repeat his death and resurrection in the contemporary disciples. One cannot write church history, therefore, with the same sense of the self-explanatory character of events with which Thucydides wrote his *Peloponnesian Wars*. The history of the Christian church is paradoxically the history of the presence of something past.[5] It is useless, said Luther, simply to preach a history or chronicle. For faith is awakened only when it is told us why Christ has come and what he has given to you and me.[6]

[4] *Histoire et Esprit*, Paris, Aubier, 1950, p. 207.
[5] Gerhard Ebeling, *Kirchengeschichte als Geschichte der Auslegung der Heiligen Schrift*, Tübingen, J.C.B. Mohr, 1947, p. 26.
[6] *Weimar Ausgabe* 7; 29, 7-17. 9; 554, 16-19. I am indebted for the Luther

How without the use of historical facts do you gauge the truth or falsehood of the Christian faith? One ought not ask of the Christian faith, "Is it true?" There is no criterion outside the paradigmatic event by which to determine the answer. One asks, "Is it meaningful?" One asks the question about meaning out of the fundamental needs of his life. The moment one does this, the concept of history as something past dwindles. With eschatological history the past loses its unique precedence in history. Past events survive only as one's future, galvanizing him into decision in the present. "Man's world seen from his own standpoint is a different course of history than history seen as a process within the stable world."[7] One hears the story of Jesus Christ and the early church as out of the past, and either it suddenly becomes the story of one's own life or it remains in the dead past. The historical consciousness of common sense asks the question, "How did it come about?" But as Karl Löwith has said, the modern historical consciousness has learned from the Bible to ask, "How shall we go about it." The remembrance of things past in Christianity does more than develop calloused hands on archeologists; it pierces the hands of man with the stigmata of the Christ.

> If Christ is born a thousand times in Bethlehem
> But not in you, you still remain eternally lost.
> —(ANGELUS SILESIUS)

History which is not made with scientific scruples cannot be appropriated with scientific scruples. The technological reason must give way to the historical reason. As Albert Camus says, "Historical reason is an irrational and romantic form of reason, which sometimes recalls the false logic of the insane and the mystic affirmation of the word, of former times."[8] As soon, for instance, as the man Bacon gets the better of Bacon the scientist,

---

references to Gerhard Ebeling's *Evangelische Evangelienauslegung, eine Untersuchung zu Luthers Hermeneutik,* Munich, Evangelischer, 1942.

[7] Gerhard Krüger, *op. cit.,* p. 14.

[8] *Op. cit.,* p. 191.

Bacon refuses to stand back from the flame to study the chemical properties of fire at a distance. He thrusts his hand in the flame to feel its elements intimately. While Flaubert writes his account of the poisoning of Madame Bovary, he suffers two attacks of indigestion and vomits his entire dinner. When van Gogh wishes to depict the sun, he does not sketch its architectural roundness as a Leonardo might. He squeezes the yellow tube on the canvas and resolutely presses out the depth with his pallet knife. Some modern painters have been known even to take the thick paint into their mouths, spit it on the canvas, and spread it with their tongues. History is, as Dilthey says, "the autobiography of the human spirit." It is nothing one can hold away from the rest of his life, for history is the person living. Nothing happens in the Christian faith that is not meant to happen for man. There is no knowledge of God which is not at the same time historical knowledge, that is, knowledge of oneself. Hence the Christian man does not live in time as a sailor in a boat. He does not even dredge up islands of meaning out of the inundated past. Man is himself an historical being. He lives in time as a fish in water. He is in time, but time is in him. And, to quote the poet Baudelaire,

> Time eats up all things alive.
> Time blots me out as flakes on freezing waters fall.
> Time is the gambler that need not cheat to win.

"Avid for life and driven wild by tedium,"[9] man lives in time like a fish in water, moment by moment straining out his means of livelihood from that "sea of lost illusions,"[10] until he comes upon the Christ who in time is the Lord of time. And in his dying he begins to live again. He eavesdrops on the story of Adam and does not ask, "Did it really happen?" He rather whirls in his tracks and says through smoldering eyes, "You called my name." He hears the story of Jesus Christ and falling to his knees he cries, "He saved

[9] *Flowers of Evil*, tr. by George Dillon and Edna St. Vincent Millay, Harpers, 1936, pp. 207, 251, 255, 37-8.
[10] As Krüger calls history, *op. cit.*, p. 19.

my life." This is the mood of the Christian apprehension of truth. The Christian does not find a fact in time which hinges together past with future. He is found as one who is hinged pathetically to a past that pulls him down, and who is turned about in an inexplicable *metanoia* which hinges him anew to a source of hope.

It is not given to a Christian to say whether his faith is true or false, but to believe in his heart that God raised Jesus from the dead, and to confess with his mouth that Jesus is Lord. (Romans 10:9) When one has met this Christ across the arithmetical expanse of time and felt his life hinged to the author of life, he can know he has come upon "time's other dimension of depth and inwardness,"[11] where history has a future. As our Lord has said, "He who hears my word and believes Him who sent me, *has* eternal life; he does not come into judgment, but has passed from death to life." (John 5:24)

How does Christology escape docetism in this setting? Docetism is the ancient heresy that presents Christ as only apparently historical, whereas classical Christianity holds Christ to be really and fully historical. To say that the word became flesh means that Jesus Christ as the presence of God was an historical reality. It is being widely said today that any lack of stress upon the historicity of Jesus Christ is a renewal of the ancient heresy of docetism. By historicity is usually meant not only that Jesus Christ was a real participant in world history but that the factuality of his existence can be determined. If that cannot be said, so the argument goes, docetism is imminent.

If that *is* said, my conviction would be that docetism has already been committed. Indeed, to say Christ is historical *does* mean now what it once meant to say "the word became flesh." It does *not* mean that Christ once lived in world history. "Flesh" does not refer to Christ's calculable displacement value in the world. That would be the most vapid and innocuous vulgarity. To say Christ is historical, the word become flesh, is to say he has

[11] Gabriel Marcel, *The Mystery of Being*, Vol. I, Regnery, 1950, p. 197.

entered fully into the conditions of our life in order to provide the conditions for our eternal life. To say he is historical means he is the event in which all history finds the form of its existence. Therefore, to harp on his historicity as if that meant his factual past is to truncate his historicity by cutting him out of our history, the very history he came to constitute. In the setting of today's historiography it is the historicists who are committing docetism.

Considering contemporary historiography, a docetist is one who does not accept Christ paradigmatically, does not make the Christ event the form of his existence. In the moment of attempting to establish the existence of Jesus as a figure in world history, the historicist suspends the place of Christ as the paradigmatic event, and abridges his full historicity. That is docetism.

Does not this view discount the incarnation, which says God entered human time in Christ? On the contrary, is it not a superficial view of Christ to identify his humanity with the spectacle of this world's time? For the time which Christ entered is not the time that we project upon the orderly spaces of calendar and clock, but the time of our life which Christ enters is the time of deadlines, and that time killed him as it is now killing us. It is the time of decision, a dimension deep below that thin film of statistically ordered time which glosses over the abyss beneath each fleeting moment. It is the time we *are* before we count the time we *have*. That time is the time in which we either meet the Lord of time or perish.

Chronological, successive time is a cultural invention, a febrile epiphenomenon. Christ does enter that time. That is part of his humiliation, but only an accidental part. Chronological time is the last courageous cough of a life that has no ultimate time within itself. It is the smoked glass which hides the hideous truth that our end is not a long way off, not even at an actuarial distance. For our end is now, where meaning in God abuts our aimless, evanescent course, forcing the choice which sets our very destiny.

The time of man is a sinking hole from which extends no stairway of escape. Into *that* time Christ has his mission. He does not simply brush across the surface of our cultivated world. He plunges deep into the *bowels* of time, the turbulence beneath our fabricated calm, there to reveal that we need not be at our end because he has become our end and there is hope in him. The time which Christ enters, then, is not alone the filmy, factual ordinary time on everybody's lips when asked. It is subliminal time, where lives are running out, like rivers without edges—the time of lived profundity where ultimate attachments form and life is hinged to destinies or else unhinged to drift to doom. That is the time of history where all our petty times resolve in wholeness. That is the time Christ enters, and by his advent sets within our reach the hope that never terminates because it terminates our hopelessness.

CHAPTER

8

THE REALITY
OF THE RESURRECTION

THE question of the historicity of Christ is the question of his paradigmatic and eschatological role in history. His advent in history creates the possibility for history in God's presence. He is historical, therefore, in the sense that he becomes the source for the final form of human existence. If that is the case, the even more delicate question of the historicity of his resurrection is involved. There more than anywhere theology is forced to choose its historiographical tools with care. For a mishandling of the historical reality of the resurrection could thwart the realization of the very history which his living presence is given to precipitate.

The resurrection is the presence of the exalted Christ, who inaugurates eschatological history and becomes its "first fruit." That is the significance attaching to the resurrection in the New Testament preaching (kerygma). Not all references to the resurrection in the New Testament are kerygmatic, however. Some are mythological. That is not to say that the resurrection is mythological, but simply that it is sometimes treated mythologically in New Testament literature.

Resurrection myths appear in the New Testament when the eschatological event is discussed as though it were world history. When the reality of the resurrection is treated as an event in world history, the preaching concern of the New Testament is ob-

189

structed, blocking the resurrection as the source and first-fruits of eschatological history. An interpretation of the resurrection which would be consistent with the Christian intention would be a process of reading the New Testament in such a way as to give the kerygma precedence over the myth. That is what Rudolf Bultmann means by "demythologizing." As such, demythologizing is not a negative thing. It is the positive process of interpreting the resurrection in order to allow it to become a reality in the present. Myth is not to be stripped away from the Bible. It is rather the kerygma that is to be separated from the myth. In the process, the preaching is given paramountcy in the exegesis of the New Testament and in the faith of the church. This process cannot be entered into fairly, however, until a number of concepts used in the discussion —concepts already bulky with emotional connotation and conflicting definitions—are clarified.

The most ambiguous yet most central of these concepts is history. History is an ambiguous concept because we are accustomed to think that Christianity is historical and by historical we have meant something that has happened and is past. Every dictionary definition supports that meaning and popular Christianity's understanding of history is identical with the dictionary definition. The church has a right to know what the theologians know: when Christianity is pressed into that dictionary definition it is being mythologized. To demythologize, therefore, one must de-historicize what Christian people feel is necessarily world history, and this seems destructive of the faith. Actually, however, the Christian's reference is not to the world's past, for Christianity is kerygmatic. By that is meant that Christianity is something which is happening now, hence not a myth, not a story about something located in past history. To de-historicize, then, does not mean to cease referring to Christianity as historical but to elevate the historical reference into the dimension of eschatological history.

The concept of kerygma becomes ambiguous when used in this way, for one has been accustomed to think that kerygma is a body of sayings which the historical scholar can identify in the Bible as the earliest form of Christian communication. Or the kerygma may be the act of witnessing or pointing to the truth about God. But when one refers to the kerygma as the total event in which the living God makes himself real in the church, the ambiguity begins to make itself felt. Some patient analysis is required at this point, for the moment this sense of kerygma is neglected, mythologizing threatens to set in.

But then the concept of the myth becomes ambiguous. The popular view is that myth is something untrue; hence one hesitates to say there is myth in the New Testament. In more sophisticated literary and philosophical circles, moreover, myth is the necessary expression of truths too deep to be scientifically appropriated. In that sense, one does not get the truth of a myth except through the use of the myth. In the study of the history of religion, however, myth is defined in quite a different way, resulting in a great deal of confusion in current theological discussion. Myth is the way in which religions refer to their Gods as though they were actors in world history. Through a process of oral and literary communication, the Gods become historicized in mythology. In the particular case of Christianity, the historicizing of the revelation of God is not the necessary medium for the expression of the truth of God, for in apostolic times kerygma was an earlier form of Christian expression than myth and its power to create history was more efficient.

Mythological expression, therefore, is neither necessary nor false. Because the kerygma renders the myth superfluous, the myth is not necessary, but because the myth retains the intention of the preaching, the myth is not false. Nevertheless, myth obscures preaching because of the way in which for the hearer it takes on the status of verifiable world history. The reality of the resurrection occurs in the preaching of the church. That is why demythologizing is inseparable from the responsibility of a theology which appreciates the eschatological dimension of history.

The belief in the resurrection is not just one among many Christian beliefs. It is the controlling center of the Christian faith. It is the meaning of the presence of God in history and the first-fruit of the eschatological age. If the resurrection is the heart, and if one demythologizes it, what remains of the body of faith when one is through? Demythologizing is not a denial of the resurrection. Nor is it the attributing of the resurrection stories to valid but fictionalized ideas in the mind of the primitive church. It is rather the effort to liberate the preaching of the resurrection from a misleading historiography known as myth. Demythologizing is in that sense the choice of kerygma as the historiography through which the faith of the church is kept alive.

I. THE ESCHATOLOGICAL EVENT

The resurrection is "not an event of past history."[1] This position which is now branding Rudolf Bultmann as dangerous was taken by Karl Barth more than a quarter of a century ago. On the strength of it, Barth became the leading evangelical spokesman in our time. More recently, in reviewing Bultmann's project, Barth has said that for Bultmann the resurrection is not historical fact in the sense of being ascertainable by the means and methods of modern science. "In that he is entirely right," Barth concedes; "no one would deny that."[2]

"No one would deny that" if by "no one" is meant the sophisticated historiographers of modern times who generally assert with Goethe and Nietzsche that there are no facts but only interpretations. Barth is equally right if he has in mind the reformers' attitude toward history. It is "not sufficient to know only the bare history . . . ," Luther claimed, "for where only the history is preached, it is a frivolous preaching and without fruit."[3] Or, to cite Calvin, faith is not based on "history which, when told of

---

[1] *Kerygma and Myth*, S.P.C.K., 1954, p. 42.
[2] *Die kirchliche Dogmatik*, III, 2, p. 535.
[3] *Sermons*, Edinburgh, p. 397.

Christ, is taken to be true, nor on reports narrated from the past. Such does not merit the name faith."[4]

Is it true, however, that no one would deny that the resurrection is not history if the character of the New Testament documents is kept in mind and if the way the church through its development has held these documents? Is it not rather as Goguel has said, that the resurrection narratives "assumed the character of a factual history which can be proved true and must be believed if one is to be saved?" Did not a myth-making historiography intervene between the original event of the resurrection and the writing of the story, giving to the story a world-historical character it did not intrinsically intend?[5] Is it not fully as true that the church at large is consciously informed more by the insinuation of the sheer factuality of the resurrection implicit in the New Testament stories than it is by the theologians' interpretive refinements? As David Friedrich Strauss once candidly observed, "By the church the evangelical narratives are received as history," hence, "to the church all those premises are wanting on which the theologian rests his . . . conclusions."[6]

If the churches knew why the resurrection is not history in the popularly conceived, world-historical sense, that understanding would promote health in the church. The gap between the unreflective body of Christians and the critical theologians, which is constantly producing an inflammation in the body of Christ, would be overcome. Strauss knew that his own kind of answers would only be salt in the wound, so he offered several compromises with the astringent truth: capitulate to the churches, leave the ministry and become a professor (he endorsed neither), or feign the position of the churches when speaking to them, while actually only drawing morals from the text.[7]

[4] *Calvini opera selecta*, edited by Peter Barth, Vol. I, p. 69 from the 1536 edition of *The Institutes*, Munich, 1926.
[5] Cf. Maurice Goguel, *The Birth of Christianity*, p. 65.
[6] *The Life of Jesus*, Vol. III, 1846 edition, pp. 441, 442.
[7] Strauss elected this tongue-in-cheek compromise. Schleiermacher had carried

Bultmann endorses no such compromise. At least in this sense he is no Strauss *redivivus*, not because he is more honorable, but because his critical study of New Testament literature and his exegesis based upon it neither require nor allow such a compromise. He has taken the problem directly to the churches. Without trying simply to protect the integrity of the theologian, he has raised the question of the integrity of a church which holds its beliefs as it does. For the resurrection is not past history, not because it is not real and not because it did not happen. It is the most real of all happenings and it is the source of the life of the church. But its uniqueness inheres in the kind of event it is. "God speaks to us not out of history, but through Christ who is the revelation of history."[8] Or, as Dibelius says it, "What founded Christianity was not knowledge about an historical process, but the confidence that the content of the story was salvation and the decisive beginning of the end."[9] The resurrection is an eschatological event, hence beyond world history, but beyond world history in such a way as to give all history its end, its limit, its destiny, its ultimate sense, its salvation, its "freedom to live one's life out of the invisible."[10] If the church does not know that this is what the New Testament is really saying, then it is in the position of holding its faith somewhat faithlessly.

An eschatological event means at least four things, and these are four ways of saying why the resurrection is not world history.

---

through a similar compromise with pre-eminent success as a preacher. A cursory reading of his sermons will show that. If the theologian follows Strauss' advice, when he preaches about the resurrection, "He will indeed set out from the sensible fact of the resurrection of Christ, but he will dwell chiefly on the being buried and rising again with Christ, which the Apostle himself has strenuously inculcated." *Ibid. cit.*, p. 444

[8] *Urchristentum*, p. 209. Cf. *Kerygma and Myth*, p. 111. Cf. comment on the Pauline usage, "from this time on" in Bultmann's *Exegetische Probleme des Zweiten Korinther-briefe*, Uppsala, 1947, p. 17, where it is stated that the resurrection is real objectively, not just subjectively in conversion. It is appropriated and realized only in faith.

[9] *From Tradition to Gospel*, p. 295

[10] *Kerygma und Mythos*, Vol. I, p. 45.

1. It is not a visible, but an invisible event. That is, the resurrection as an eschatological event is not apparent to objective research and empirical investigation. It does not deal with facts whose validity can be demonstrated. Bultmann is therefore right to say, "The resurrection, of course, simply cannot be a visible fact in the realm of human history."[11]

2. The eschatological event of the resurrection is not an event in world time, in chronological time, but rather an event having to do with one's personal life and the life of the eschatological community, the church. It is the "now" of John 12:31 which is not of the world because it comes into the world as the world's limit and hope. It is a cosmic event in the respect that it affects the whole world, yet it is not in world time.[12] If it were in empirical time, it would be one event alongside the event of the crucifixion. But as an eschatological event, it is co-present with the cross as the dimension of salvation in the cross. It is the deed of God in which the cross becomes an holy event. It is the meaningfulness of the cross.[13] The cross and the faith-claims of the disciples are past history, although one need make no effort to certify them as such. But the resurrection not only is not an historical event in the world history of the past; it should not primarily stir up an interest in the past. Jesus' "ministry was not understood as a decisive event for Israel's history like the call of

11 *Theology of the New Testament*, Scribners, Vol. I, p. 295.
12 Karl Barth has given me access to an unpublished letter he received from Bultmann in response to Barth's *Rudolf Bultmann, ein Versuch ihn zu Verstehen*. In the letter, Bultmann adduces the following references in support of his claim about the cosmic character of the Christ event: Rom. 5:12 ff., 1 Cor. 15:22 ff. (especially 20 ff., but not 1 Cor. 15:5-8); Col. 2:12, Eph. 2:6. Professor Bultmann has granted me permission to quote from this letter.
13 *Kerygma and Myth*, p. 112; *Kerygma und Mythos*, Vol. I, p. 47. The Greek word for "cross" is not used in the Gospel of John as a particular holy event. The word does not even appear in Jesus' sayings or in John's letters. Rather the word "to lift up, to exalt" is used which has the significance of resurrection. *Das Evangelium des Johannes*, p. 490, note 5.

Moses, the exodus from Egypt, the giving of the Law on Sinai, or God's raising up of kings and prophets. . . . Neither in the earliest Church nor anywhere in the New Testament is Jesus looked back upon as a deed of God. . . . For Jesus' importance as Messiah-Son-of-Man lies not at all in what he did in the past, but entirely in what is expected of him for the future."[14]

3. The eschatological event of the resurrection is not a past, but a future event. By calling it future, one need not rehabilitate the concept of chronological time. An event is in the future if we have no warrant for it in advance of the attitude we take toward it. Any appeal to a certainty prior to the decision of faith would be a violation of the meaning of justification by faith which is the saving content of the cross. The case for this can be illuminated from two directions. First, from the exegetical standpoint, the gospels are written entirely from the point of view of the resurrection. (John 2:22) Hence, to appeal to the narratives leading up to the event of the resurrection as if they were prior clues to its possibility is an exegetical anachronism.

Second, the case can be illuminated from the direction of Heidegger's philosophy. Heidegger strips the concepts of past, present, and future of their linear, chronological meaning. The past in his philosophy means the realm of inauthenticity, our brute location in the world. The future means the realm of possibility and authenticity where our destiny is being determined. The present in most philosophies has had no status but for the mathematical point in the transition from the future into the past. In Heidegger's philosophy, the present is the realm of *Mitsein*—or being-with—the realm of personal presence. As Kierkegaard has said, in the presence of the person of God, the dimension of the present is for the first time given real substance. With God in our future, we have redemption from the inauthenticity of the past, so that our present which is a being in his presence is full with meaning. The resur-

[14] *Theology of the New Testament*, Vol. I, p. 36.

rection is the presence of God in Jesus Christ. Hence, it is an eschatological event. That means it is an event entirely future because it is determining the ultimate destiny of history in a way that nothing in the past could do it. We are not to know Christ as something which is past, therefore. We are grasped by him as that which is coming toward us in the resurrection.

It may seem that the word "future" is being used in more than one sense throughout this discussion. That is true, for there is more than one kind of future. There is the future which exists at a chronological distance, and there is the future as the experience of a present which is saved from vanishing into the past because of the imminent presence of another reality. English suffers theologically from having only one word for two meanings. The Japanese language, for instance, has two words for future to accommodate this distinction. *Mirai* means "what has not yet come" and *shorai* means "what is imminent." According to Seiichi Hatano, "In Japanese philosophy people usually mix these words without thinking. We must be careful to distinguish them."[15]

The German language, famous for its theological flexibility, was first forced to honor this distinction when it became the successor to Latin as the medium for theological reflection. Latin theology used two words which carried quite different connotations concerning the future, namely, *futurum* and *adventus*. *Futurum* most clearly meant that which exists at a chronological distance. Any peasant would have chosen *Zukunft* as its equivalent. But the original etymological sense of *Zu-kunft* was identical with *adventus*, "what is coming toward us." The writings of Luther, for instance, abound in the use of *Zukunft* with reference to meanings which have no possible relationship to a *futurum*.[16] In contemporary theology, Bultmann and Gogarten, following Luther and

<hr>

[15] *Time and Eternity* (*Toki to eien*), *Collected Works*, Vol. V, Tokyo, 1949, p. 12.

[16] Cf. the etymological discussion in Arthur Rich, *Die Bedeutung der Eschatologie für den christlichen Glauben*, Zürich, 1954, pp. 4-6.

Heidegger, have built a large case upon this distinction. The unique element in the Christian view of history for them is precisely its future, its eschatological character. The resurrection is future in just this *zu-künftig* sense. As all Christian phenomena, as all elements in the dimension of eschatological history it is "that which is coming toward us, concerning which we know nothing except that it comes to us."[17] The resurrection is the reality by virtue of whose imminence we do not know it as we know other realities. But by virtue of that same imminence, its presence saves our present from slipping into the past of nothingness, inauthenticity, or death.

4. The eschatological event of the resurrection is not an answer to the question "how" but to the question "why." The resurrection, that is, does not pertain to a picture of the world but to one's self-understanding. As Bultmann has said to Barth in a private letter, the weakness of our time, indeed of the last two centuries, has been the effort to relate Christianity to an objective world-view without self-understanding.

I was reminded of this problem one evening when I heard my wife ask my children, "Would you like to hear the story of how Jesus was born?" I interrupted with a stricture from Bultmann. I said, "But my dear, the thing to be known about the birth of Jesus is not *how* but *why* he was born." My wife replied with an innocence which remains the plague of the theologian, "I was only going to read what the Bible says!"

The Bible undeniably hints *how* Jesus was born and comes very close to telling *how* Jesus was raised from the dead. It is as if the birth of Jesus were the genetic consequence of the wedding of God with Israel and as if the resurrection of Jesus were a cosmographic vindication of realities immanent in the life and ministry of Jesus. Is this not the misleading thing about the Gospels which a reading of the Epistles helps to correct? Ought not the critical study of the

[17] Gogarten, *Der Mensch zwischen Gott und Welt*, p. 389; *Verhängnis und Hoffnung der Neuzeit*, pp. 122-4.

historiographies employed in the development of the gospel tradition from kerygma to myth provide a clue to that historical materialism? The story of the resurrection as it is given in the New Testament is the story of an eschatological event which appears first and in its purest form in the faith and preaching of the apostles. In the course of telling the story and in the eventual recording of the story, the eschatological event became obscured by a process of mythologizing. Myth is the process of treating the eschatological event as world history, treating as past what is really future, treating as visible what is invisible, binding to the public history of the past what is really the prophetic and personal history of God's presence "with us." The story of how the resurrection tradition became a literary gospel is the story of how the kerygma became mythologized.

On what basis is such a judgment made? On the basis that even within the written gospels and within the other documents of the New Testament there is discernible an original *kerygma* which stands in judgment upon the latterly developed mythology. This is why demythologizing is indicated in the very nature of the myth itself. Myth points to a mode of communication purer than itself. To say it as Bultmann docs, using a term best known to phenomenological philosophy, "The *intention* of the myth is the kerygma." "Exegesis should not, then, simply reproduce the myth; it must rather attempt to advance to the proper intention of the text."[18]

II. COMPARATIVE HISTORIOGRAPHIES

The proper intention of the New Testament text is preaching. While myth tends to embed the resurrection in past history, kerygma returns it to its proper status as eschatological event where it can confront us in the present. In that sense, preaching is as 2nd Peter calls it, "the prophetic word," the very antithesis of myth. (1:19) The *concept* of a myth appears explicitly in only a few places in the New Testament, but where it does appear, it means

[18] *Glauben und Verstehen*, Vol. I, p. 208, n. 1.

something obviously hostile to the Christian truth, something "cunningly devised." (2 Peter 1:16) The striking thing about these few references is that in each case the preaching of the word is commended as the proper antidote to myth. (2 Tim. 4:4; 1 Tim. 1:4; Titus 1:14)

a. *Preaching or Myth?* Preaching is the announcement of God's presence in Christ. As such, it bridges the gap from the faith of the apostles to our faith. The faith of the apostles, of course, is not a doctrine, not a dogmatic datum, but an experience of transition from death to life in response to the living person of Jesus Christ. Preaching communicates this living relation. It is the conviction of the Apostle Paul that when he propagates the word he propagates the life. The New Testament preaching is always evoking the either/or decision between life and death which is present in the living Lordship of the resurrected one. "Belief in the resurrection, and the faith that Christ himself, yes God himself, speaks in the proclaimed word (2 Cor. 5:20) are identical." (Bultmann)[1]

The content of the Easter preaching is simply that "God has made the prophet and teacher Jesus of Nazareth Messiah!" The short proclamation in Romans 4:25 is regarded by Bultmann as "a pattern of the Christological kerygma": he was "put to death for our trespasses, raised for our justification."[2] "If Christ be not risen, our faith is in vain." The proper paraphrase of that verse would be, according to Bultmann, "If Christ is not present in the preaching, in the faith, in the event, he is a mythical form."[3]

The preaching, then, is inseparable from the resurrection and the resurrection from the preaching. For the resurrection is God's speech in Christ, which inaugurates the new age. The preaching is the speech of Christ through the church and is the sign and power

---

[1] *Theology of the New Testament*, Vol. I, p. 305, 2 Cor. 2:14-6:10. Cf. *Der Begriff der Offenbarung im N.T.*, p. 27, and *Exegetische Probleme des zweiten Korintherbriefes*, e.g., p. 20, "the apostolic preaching is of a piece with the *Heilsgeschehen*," the holy event.
[2] *New Testament Theology*, Vol. I, p. 43; and pp. 83 ff.
[3] From Bultmann's private letter to Karl Barth.

of the new age. The prototype of all preaching is God's word to man in the exaltation of Christ on the cross. God speaks in the cross and man hears in the resurrection: This is the single event of God's proclamation. The hyphenation of speaking-hearing, of cross-resurrection, *is* the eschatological event. It includes God's merciful act and man's response of faith. It includes dying and rising. This responsibility for preaching is passed on to the church. Now we have Christ's ministry. We are Christ's ambassadors. God spoke in Christ. His living speech is the eschatological event which becomes present in the speech of preaching.

On the other hand, myth cloaks kerygma in such a way as to conceal it. Myth muffles the voice of the resurrection. Myth simply sketches the impulses of the sound of preaching like a theological applause meter, but straining out the acoustical properties. Myth is a seismographic account of the thunder that marks the place where God once spoke, but its power to let God speak again is in question. While preaching recreates the eschatological event, myth buries the event in narratives which indicate the past. The empty tomb stories are in this sense marks not so much of the resurrection as of the mythologizing of the resurrection. This is why, as Luther said, the angels were good preachers. When the apostles fixed their gaze upon the empty tomb, the angels said, "He is risen," by which they meant, "on earth, which is the realm of death, you must not seek Christ."

Myth in this sense is not the "cunningly devised" myth which was more conspicuous to the early church. The formation of the resurrection myths was not a laborious or logical process but a spontaneous response to the kerygma. As Bultmann noted very early in his studies, "The Easter event in distinction from other kinds of legends in the New Testament grew out of the Christian faith and worship rather than out of judaistic or hellenistic motives."[4] The main exception to this is, of course, the use and defense of what Bultmann calls "the original Iranian presentation of the

[4] *Geschichte der synoptischen Tradition*, 1st edition, Göttingen, 1921, p. 184.

resurrection."[5] Other exceptions are found, on the one hand, in the spatial localization of the resurrection as a linear philosophy of history contributed by Jewish apocalypticism, and, on the other hand, in the gnostic notion of a pre-existent divine being. But the general characteristic in the mythologizing of the resurrection is dependent upon no particular prior body of mythology. It simply manifests the historiographical method characteristic of all mythologizing, that is, historicizing into world history an eschatological event which really is not past history.

b. *The Evangelical Decision.* Kerygma and myth can be seen, then, as two kinds of historiography. Myth is the cautious, protective, conservative concern to preserve the record of God's dealing with man, as if God's acts were as accessible to the public as any event in world history. Preaching proceeds with little regard to the question of past factualities because its concern is with transcending world history in the movement toward eschatological history.

The choice between these historiographies, therefore, is of the greatest magnitude for the integrity of the gospel in the church. One of the great enigmas of the Church Year is what occurs from the pulpits of churches on Easter Sunday morning. From Advent to Easter there is a mounting crescendo in the worship of the church, quite authentically reflected in the color and gaiety of life around us at Easter time. What, then if the preacher at the climax enunciates incredulous apologetics about the "historicity" of the resurrection? People who have come with the expectancy of being swept up into the joy and excitement of the new age in Christ, could be turned away wondering how intelligent men can say such things. What is even worse, they could be led to accept the resurrection as a fact of the past and thereby miss the resurrection as a future, an imminent presence which supports their life in the present.

[5] As in Mark 12:18-27 and 1 Cor. 15. *Vide* Bultmann's article on *mythos* in *Religion in Geschichte und Gegenwart,* 2nd edition.

Several Easters ago *The New York Times* reported the following statements from the Sermons of a Catholic priest, an Episcopal Bishop, and a Congregational pastor: " 'That our Lord arose glorious and immortal is a historical fact that cannot be overthrown.' " "The Resurrection was 'a historical fact. How this happened, no man can say. But that it did happen, no one who honors historical evidence can doubt.' " "What happened on Easter was 'the one absolute, incontrovertible unanswerable proof that Christianity is true.' " (Monday, April 2, 1956) That kind of language is not preaching; it is mythology. An unwitting conspiracy against the vitality of the church's life is nursed in its bosom, diverting one from the dimension of eschatological history, which is the church's sole claim to a mission.

Further to clarify the seriousness of this evangelical decision, the relation of kerygma and myth may be stated more precisely in terms of the New Testament resurrection materials.

1. Preaching communicates the resurrection invisibly; myth makes it visible. Mythologizing is a process of visualizing the kerygma, a process conterminous with the development of the gospel as a literary form. All the resurrection narratives which appeal to the visibility of the resurrected Lord participate in this myth-making tendency.[6]

Bultmann differs from others such as Barth on the meaning of the resurrection miracles in the same way in which Luther differs from Calvin and the scholastics. Barth, for instance, takes an ambivalent attitude toward the miracle stories which visualize the resurrection. On the one hand, he explains away elements which Bultmann believes were literally meant.[7] On the other hand, Barth

---

[6] Cf. Strauss' amusing illustrations in *New Life of Jesus*, Vol. I, pp. 207, 208.
[7] Of the Epistle of John where it is said that the apostles preach what they have "seen, heard, and felt," (I John 1:2) Barth dexterously asserts that the apostle is referring to the life-time acquaintance with Jesus and not to the resurrection acquaintance. *Die kirchliche Dogmatik*, III, 2, p. 529. In the same way but equally to the dissatisfaction of Bultmann, Barth explains

takes his stand with Calvin in regarding the miracle stories not as proofs but as indispensable signs.[8] For Calvin, the presence of earthquakes, angels, and nail-marked hands after the resurrection is God's way, as Calvin says, of pulling the ears of the apostles, "that they might remain no longer in sluggishness and despair." "When he makes known by outward signs that he is present, he invites us to him."[9]

Miracle in this sense Bultmann would classify as myth or *Mirakel*, for it visualizes, historicizes, and hence competes with the eschatological miracle which is the Christ event, the *Wunder*. Barth, then, could well charge here, as he does in his little writing on Bultmann, that Bultmann has only one fault: "He is a Lutheran." For Bultmann adopts Luther's and not Calvin's attitude toward miracle. According to Luther, the *Word* is the saving miracle. This is why Luther deplores Philip's asking for a sign before believing. "Philip counteth it not sufficient to believe the Word, but goeth about to come to the knowledge of the Father by another means than the word." Christ appeared visibly but once, namely, in his lifetime. Hereafter, says Luther, he is visible only in his word, the preaching.[10] Then Luther tells of how he once saw a vision of Christ. He ordered it away because it was of the devil. Luther and Bultmann appear to be in agreement with the Apostle Paul. The decisive sign that Christ is risen and that the

---

that Paul's roll of witnesses to the resurrection in 1 Cor. 15 implies not Paul's purpose to "confirm the fact of the resurrection of Jesus, not for that purpose at all, but to confirm that the foundation of the church, so far as the eye can see, can be traced back to nothing else than the appearances of the risen Christ." *The Resurrection of the Dead*, p. 143. Bultmann, on the other hand, can only see in this passage "the attempt to make the resurrection of Christ believable as an objective, historical fact." *Glauben und Verstehen*, Vol. I, p. 54. But he finds Paul internally inconsistent because what he says in verses 20 to 22 cannot be said of an historical fact.

[8] "The empty grave and ascension are signs of the Easter event." *Op. cit.*, III, 2, p. 543.

[9] *Harmony of the Evangelists*, p. 344.

[10] *Sermons*, p. 294; *Table Talk*, ccxxxvi.

new age is upon us is not to be found in the resurrection miracle stories, but "in the fact that Christ is being preached."[11]

2. Preaching communicates a saving event; myth locates this event in chronological time. Myth objectifies the divine event and projects it into world history. It is in this regard that the apocalyptic mythology of Judaism, such as appears in the Book of Daniel has influenced the apostolic preaching of the resurrection, making of the eschatological event of Christ's resurrection a philosophy of world history.[12] This method of mythologizing is familiar to religion in general as the practice of "the objectification of the divine in space-time and human images." (Tillich)[13]

Was it not precisely the apocalyptic myth of Judaism which tempted the New Testament preacher to see the resurrection of Jesus as a point in world history? But the *preaching* of the resurrection is to an historicized Christianity what the preaching of the prophets was to Israel: an exposure of every effort at confusing God and world history. (cf. Isaiah 14 and Ezekiel 29) Israel was inhospitable to myth not because Israel was an historical community, but because it was a monotheistic community which knew that God does not "appear" in history. The Christian community is inhospitable to myth not because Christianity is rooted in historical facts, but because it is the ambassador of the resurrected Christ, the eschatological event which does not depend upon the world but rather creates the new age.

It is possible to prefer the gnostic myth to the myth of Judaism, for the gnostics believed the world was alien to divine reality. The Old Testament faith knew of God as creator and therefore knew of the world as the stage of the divine drama. It did not have so radical a sense of the alienation of God and the world; hence it

[11] Cf. 2 Cor. 4:7-16. *Glauben und Verstehen*, Vol. I, p. 211.
[12] Cf. Bultmann's criticism of Cullmann and Stauffer at this point in "Heilsgeschichte und Geschichte," *Theologische Literaturzeitung*, 1948, no. 11, p. 663.
[13] Article on "Mythos" in *Religion in Geschichte und Gegenwart*, 2nd edition.

was relatively unrestrained about finding God in acts of world history. The resurrection faith of the New Testament radicalizes the transcendence of the source of our life and its non-worldly character. In that respect, Bultmann could be justified in claiming that the New Testament is closer to Gnosticism than even to the Old Testament.[14]

The stories about Easter which emphasize its occurrence on "the third day" participate in Judaistic apocalypticism, as if the resurrection were bound by some such chronological plan as appears in the Book of Daniel. The resurrection in the preaching is joined to the crucifixion not by calendar time but by eschatological, redemptive meaning. At least three elements in the New Testament account help to support this view. The first, and the most impressive of all is the rejection of the apocalyptic myth in the Johannine Gospel and Letters. The second is the Gospel of Mark, ending as it does with the witness of the centurion that "this man was a son of God" or at least with the burial of Jesus. The value of this gospel is that "the possibility of transferring the divine event into a theme of objective human history is here as good as excluded."[15] The third is found in the way in which Paul preaches the resurrection faith to the Jews *without* invoking their apocalypticism. For Paul, "the resurrection is not a grotesque, cosmic event, but the beginning of the new creation. The resurrected one is the 'first-born among many brethren' (Rom. 8:29), the second Adam (Rom. 5:12 f., 1 Cor. 15:2 f., 45). What has happened in the resurrection fulfills itself in all who believe."[16]

3. Preaching invokes a response having no support outside the decisional event. Myth makes the resurrection past, as a material basis for decision.

[14] *Glauben und Verstehen*, Vol. II, pp. 131 and 205; *Urchristentum*, pp. 183ff. Cf. Friedrich Gogarten, *The Reality of Faith*, Ch. 4. Westminster, 1959, translated by Carl Michalson et al.

[15] Gunther Dehn, *Mark*, p. 305.

[16] *Glauben und Verstehen*, Vol. I, p. 182.

In the history of religion there is what is known as the numinous encounter between man and god, but the religions have tended to express such encounters in "the stuff of a reality which is explainable to others."[17] The New Testament does not completely transcend this mythological temptation. The last word about the New Testament should elevate not its myth, however, but its kerygma. For "it is precisely its immunity from proof which secures the Christian presentation against the charge of being mythological."[18] The Christian kerygma, appealing as it does to the decision of faith without any support, saves Christianity from being classified with mythological religions.

Here the question of faith as a sacrifice of the intellect is most likely to arise. Critics of the kerygmatic historiography generally suggest that to base faith on nothing is a surrender of reason. However, in eschatological history, faith is based not on a sacrifice of intellect, but on the positive preaching, the witness of the church. This witness is a nothing, of course, in the same sense in which man's life as creature is a nothing, a life after the flesh, having no ultimate hope in itself. But preaching is a something in the same sense as the creative word of God is a something, constantly holding the transitory world from slipping back into its intrinsic nothingness. Hence, there is no support for faith outside the preaching moment, that is, outside the miracle (*Wunder*) of resurrection.

To find any other kind of support for one's faith is to commit what Paul saw to be the sin of the Jew and the Greek, which is the failure to give God the glory.[19] The Jew found support in the historical antecedents of God's culminating work. The Greek found support in metaphysical dogmas about pre-existent beings.

---

[17] Rühle's article on *mythos* in *Religion in Geschichte und Gegenwart*, 2nd edition.

[18] *Kerygma and Myth*, p. 42. Cf. *Theology of the New Testament*, Vol. I, p. 304, where myth is contrived in the New Testament to make faith easier.

[19] *Glauben und Verstehen*, Vol. I, p. 261.

These world-historical and metaphysical theologies, in their effort to support faith, really add nothing to faith. Indeed, they destroy faith. As Barth once said, "Even faith, if it proceeds from anything but a void, is unbelief."[20] Or, as a disciple of Bultmann commented recently, "When the congregations here and there so-to-say put a revolver to the chest of the pastor and require him to answer 'yes' or 'no' to the physically-conceived bodily resurrection of Jesus, one must make it clear to them that their question is dictated by unbelief."[21]

It has been instructive for me to observe student reactions scribbled in the margins of library books on the resurrection stories. Repeatedly, in places where scholarship has implied certain narratives could have no factual basis, the student has written, "Why not?" The meaning of this is clear to me. From within one's faith in the presence of God in Christ it is nothing to move to the affirmation of otherwise incredible tales about how God may have brought this all about. There is a sense in which, when we are confronted by the risen Christ, all our critical fibres go limp with credulity. One does not then seek evidence by which to confirm his faith. He rather finds his faith confirming the purported evidence. As a character in a novel wrote in her diary after experiencing her own resurrection of faith, "I believe there's a God—I believe the whole bag of tricks; there's nothing I don't believe; they could subdivide the Trinity into a dozen parts and I'd believe. They could dig up records that proved Christ had been invented by Pilate to get himself promoted, and I'd believe just the same. I've caught belief like a disease. I've fallen into belief like I fell in love."[22] The most sophisticated theologians have done the same thing with the resurrection stories.[23]

---

[20] *The Epistle to the Romans*, Oxford, 1933, pp. 56, 57.
[21] Ernst Fuchs in *Zeitschrift für Theologie und Kirche*, Jahrgang 48, Heft 3, p. 343.
[22] Graham Greene, *The End of the Affair*, Bantam, 1955, p. 126.
[23] Austin Farrer has said approvingly, "Christians accept with regard to Christ testimonies which would be inconclusive applied to any other man."

The approach to the resurrection in terms of its possibility by-passes its reality. The point about the resurrection is not whether it is possible but what kind of reality it is. One ought not ask, "Could it have happened?" but rather "What is the meaning of the event?" At this point something is lacking in the customary historiographical implication in the concept of *Heilsgeschichte*. *Heilsgeschichte* adopts what might be called a proleptic view of history. Something which becomes true for me in the present is assigned a reality which is prior to my realization of it. Prolepsis is an anachronism by which what is known only in the present is given the status of being in the past. Relative to the resurrection, then, one would be willing to agree that it is true for you only in faith, not by historical evidence. But once it is true in faith, that is, in eschatological history, is it not found to be true in world history, proleptically? Why not?

This proleptic reasoning from the faith is in a sense the spirit of the kerygmatic attitude toward faith and history, for it does not require faith to be based on history as prior evidence. But the proleptic strategy does violate the kerygmatic understanding of the way in which the object of faith is real, *extra nos*. The Christian faith is real outside us as well as within us, not because its source is identifiable at some point in human time but because it has its source in the event of God's presence. We do not first find an objective basis for belief and then believe. Neither do we, once believing, invoke an objectively historical ground for belief. We believe because the word of God calls us to decision. There is no basis for belief outside the encounter in which preaching confronts our dying flesh with the living spirit of Christ. The *extra nos* of faith is not in past history, whether positivistically or proleptically conceived, but in the everlasting rule of Christ in which "one

---

Kerygma and Myth, p. 220. Ethelbert Stauffer has said, "True history is autonomous. Nothing is impossible." *Kerygma und mythos*, Vol. II, p. 17. And Karl Barth has said concerning the resurrection narratives, "That is indeed possible. Why not?" *Die Kirchliche Dogmatik*, III, 2, p. 535.

knows he receives his life entirely from God and not from the world."[24]

4. Preaching communicates the resurrection as the meaning of existence. Myth is preoccupied with the resurrection as an independent phenomenon. Myth stands back from the resurrection event at an objective distance. The preaching pitches the resurrection into our lives as the basis for our having a history.

There is an astonishing difference in treatments of the resurrection faith as between commentaries and sermons. Commentaries, bound as they are to chapter and verse, tend to be drawn into the mythological net by the compulsion to explain and expand on every detail of the text. They tend to allow the literary method of the primitive text to dictate the structure of the Christian faith. Sermons, on the other hand, pour the entire content of the faith into the single text. They are thus spared the grave blunder of splintering the Bible into as many pieces as there are verses and of answering the concern for the bread of life with a multiplicity of exegetical stones.

John Wesley is an instructive illustration of the problem at hand. His sermons are utterly Protestant treatments of the resurrection, for he has no sermon *on* the resurrection. That is because he preaches the resurrection, bringing it to bear upon the meaning of the existence of man in such themes as "liberty from sin," "the spirit of adoption," "the first-fruits of the spirit," "the presence of the kingdom," "the righteousness of faith," and "the word of faith which we preach." If there is a central theme in the preaching of Wesley, it is the saving event, the cross-resurrection event, the new birth, the hyphenation of cross-resurrection in justification-new birth. The mythologizing of the Wesleyan preaching took place when the followers of Wesley interpreted the hyphen chronologically, as a sequence of two events in time, justification and sancti-

[24] Gerhard Ebeling, *Die Geschichtlichkeit der Kirche*, Tübingen, 1954, pp. 64, 65.

fication, rather than as one eschatological event. For as Wesley himself says in his sermon "On the New Birth," "in the order of time, neither of these is before the other." That sequence is introduced only when you reflect on and hold off at an objective distance what is really the meaning for your life.

When Wesley writes his commentary, his *Notes on the New Testament*, he does fall into the temptation of the indiscriminate emphasis, which is the temptation of the commentary. He becomes as baroque as medieval scholasticism in his treatment of the resurrection narratives. Christ is said to show his hands and feet to his disciples "that they might either see or feel the prints of the nails." (Luke 24:40) He is said to have eaten in their presence, "not that he had any need of food; but to give them still further evidence." (vs. 43) The tomb is said to have been sealed to provide God with the chance "to give the strongest proofs of Christ's ensuing resurrection."

Fortunately, the New Testament does relatively little in the way of explaining *how* Christ arose. Hence, the commentator is not excessively trapped into an analysis of the irrelevant. But the narratives of the resurrection are open to an interpretation that answers more to the how of the resurrection than to the why, more to the bizarre details than to the meaning for our salvation. Hence, they contribute to the baroque tendency in the church, which is the tendency to draw a picture where a spiritual power is indicated, to supply a *Weltbild* where a *Weltanschauung* is given. Like the flying buttresses which make a baroque thing out of a Gothic cathedral, they bind us to the earth in satisfaction of our sense of need for support and keep us out of the lofty spire from which the whole landscape of our life can be seen at a glance.

The Gospel of John demythologizes when it has Jesus say to Mary, "Touch me not." This is the gospel's own way of criticizing the extant resurrection narratives and of providing a key to the meaning of the narratives which the evangelist himself tells. It is a rebuke to the stories which emphasize touch and sight: such as, "and they came and held him by the feet, and worshipped him" (Matt. 28:9) and "handle me and see" (Luke 24:38-43). But then in the Gospel of John there are references to the post-resurrection *appearances*. Is sight in a different class from touch? Here the important thing to be noted is not the appearance itself but what Jesus directs his observer to *say* of his presence, namely, "Go to my brethren and say to them, I am ascending to my Father and your Father, to my God and your God." (John 20:17) This is the recurrent theme in the Johannine passion story. (16:28; 16:5, 10; 13:33; 14:4, 12, 28) The meaning of the resurrection, then, is—nonmythologically stated: "The father of Jesus is God! And God has become their father through him." But this meaning is "the offense of the cross" and not a faith in a "tactile, intra-worldly demonstration of the resurrected one."[25]

When Socrates was once asked if he believed a certain myth, he replied that although he could not be said to believe it, yet he was not at a loss as to its significance. While others engaged themselves in speculation as to how a citizen was carried off by a god, and of the manner of his death, Socrates simply protested that he would rather know himself. Socrates' attitude toward myth is a kind of secular paradigm of a kerygmatic historiography. The demythologizing of the resurrection is the task of a kerygmatic historiography. In the process it facilitates "the liberation of the New Testament preaching from a materialism of thought which threatens it; positively expressed, the practicing of the resurrection!"[26]

[25] Bultmann, *Das Evangelium des Johannes*, pp. 533, 534.
[26] Ernst Fuchs, *op. cit.*, p. 343. *Vide* Norman J. Young, *The Role of the Concept of History in the Theology of Rudolf Bultmann.* Unpublished doctoral dissertation, Drew University, Madison, N. J., 1959.

CHAPTER

9

THE CREATIVITY OF PREACHING

ESCHATOLOGICAL history begins where God is present with finality, in the event of Jesus Christ. The Christ event is no nature miracle. Nor is it a datum of dogmatic belief propositionally stated and institutionally enforced. Christ is a fully historical event. His resurrection is both the signal and the substance of an ultimately meaningful history. But the ability of the contemporary man to enter into that history is in a large sense dependent upon the historiographical *finesse* with which one reiterates the event. I have attempted to make the case that a kerygmatic historiography is indicated in the event of the resurrection. By that is meant that the significance of the resurrected Christ as the source of the new age is perpetuated through preaching. Preaching is historiography in an evangelical form, testifying to the good news of the eschatological event in such a way as to give rise to the eschatological history. To say it with utter simplicity, the preaching of the gospel is the telling of a story of God's turning to man in Jesus of Nazareth. In a single report it tells us to whom we really belong and saves us from being lost. Preaching is the witness to the gospel. By that witness the paratactic gaps which existential history exposes in world history are filled with the presence of God. Part of the gospel is the good news that God has appointed a people called the church for the purpose of enjoying the story and telling it to others.

It is as if Christians have witnessed a mysterious event. God has turned to man in Jesus of Nazareth, and Christians are those who have seen that this is what Jesus was about. From now on, what others will know about that event depends on whether or not some witness is willing to testify. A Christian is one who acknowledges that God has turned to man in Jesus and who takes upon himself the responsibility of turning to the world with that report. Hence, to be a Christian is to be involved in the responsibility of the communication of the gospel.

What remains, then, is the task of determining the strategy for a kerygmatic history. How shall Christians turn to the world in such a way as to supply the world with its proper end? The best answers to that question are to be found in the character of the message itself. One appeals in vain to methods of communication if they are not enlightened by the message. Public relations bureaus can catalogue every soft spot in the public's sales resistance and never have a positive suggestion for Christian communication. Writers may know every literary strategy from Aeschylus to Yeats and yet be powerless to evoke an act of Christian faith. Artists may be able to see through the surface of ordinary affairs to the turbulence and formlessness beneath, yet lack the authority to say, "Peace be still," or the one perspective that makes "all things cohere." Before the physicist Helmholtz could arrive at the nature of vision, he had to do more than study the human eye. He had to study the properties of light. Similarly, the clue to the strategy of Christian communication is best found in the nature of the message itself.

Therefore, I will single out some of the historiographical suggestions which occur in an analysis of the evangelical event and attempt to indicate how they bear upon the task of communication. It must not be thought that by preaching is meant simply what ministers do from pulpits. I am referring to any act of communication in which the intention is present to bear witness to the meaning of the Christ event for our ongoing lives.

I. NARRATION AND NEWS

The gospel is the good news about who God is and to whom, therefore, we belong. As such it speaks to our needs and longing from out of the ultimate dimension of history. It is easy to be misled about the meaning of the gospel by the fact that the first four books of the New Testament are named "gospels." The four gospels appear to be narrations of the history of Jesus' life and teachings, so that the word "gospel" takes on the connotation of a short historical narrative. The gospels are not so much histories, however, as they are propaganda contrived to elicit faith in Jesus as the revealer of God and thus to usher in the new age. They engage in evangelism, not biography; in eschatological history, not world history. "These are written that you may believe that Jesus is the Christ, the Son of God, and that believing you may have life in his name." (John 20:31) Luke, reputed historian of the evangelists, compiles the information about Christ with the intention of fostering a knowledge of its truth. (Luke 1:4)

The communication of the gospel is not directed, then, to just any question people happen to be asking. It is directed to the question about the ultimate meaning of life and a man's relation to it. As Gabriel Marcel has observed, one can spend a whole day in an art museum and appreciate nothing if he has asked the wrong questions. "Will I recognize these paintings when I see them again?" "Is this a profitable experience I am having?" The realm of beauty is dumb before such queries. A schoolboy may simply study the answers at the back of his book, as Kierkegaard points out. But he should know that in the process he will never learn to solve a problem. People who are confronting the message of Christianity with questions which the gospel is not really attempting to answer, or digging out answers to questions which they themselves have not yet asked, violate a basic condition for Christian communication, namely, that the truth about God and the truth about men involve each other.

But human questions which do not pertain to the mystery of man's ultimate significance will never open the way for the coming of the divine answers. Cervantes' Don Quixote may not be any nearer the Kingdom of Heaven simply by virtue of his painful sense of being a stranger in this world, nor Dostoevsky's Ivan by virtue of his burdening sense of guilt. But at least the gospel can be addressed to such questions of existential history. The gospel is God's answer to questions of a certain quality. "What must I do to be saved?" "Who will deliver me from the body of this death?" "Why am I something and not nothing?" It would be sheer vanity, then, to attempt to accommodate the gospel answer to other kinds of questions. It would be roughly parallel to attempting to solve lessons in French grammar by solutions at the back of an algebra text. Christians can be made to feel needlessly stupid by their quandary in the presence of the kinds of questions others raise. "Can you prove it?" "What makes you think it's better than other faiths?" "How could God create the world in six days?" "Is the Bible the inspired Word of God?" "Is a belief in bodily resurrection something we can hold today?" Christians can invent answers to any of these questions. But the answers are usually not gospel, for they do not communicate the knowledge of who God is and to whom, therefore, man belongs. They may satisfy curiosity, but they do not create history.

Not all questions are equally deserving of answers. Questions asked from mere curiosity or intellectual acquisitiveness are not the questions which draw upon the wisdom of the Christian message. Some answer to such questions should probably be given, if only in the interests of fair play. However, both parties of the dialogue should know that they are to that extent putting off the real issue. The gospel is the answer to the question men ought to be asking because of their destiny as men. And as Kierkegaard has said, it is untrue to answer a question in a medium in which it has not been asked. How ironical, then, for a Christian to prepare himself as a debater in the interests of the promulgation of the

Christian faith, only to discover his vocation to be more that of the town crier. Or consider the irony of training the Christian witness in the arts of persuasion, only to discover it is the task of the witness not to convince his hearers but "to transport them out of themselves." (Longinus)

II. WORD AND EVENTS

The gospel is the good news about God and man which comes in a certain form, the form of proclamation. Now proclamation is basically an auditory phenomenon. The witness or the preaching is an appeal more to the ear than to the eye. It was the Apostle Paul who laid down this formula. "How are they to believe in him of whom they have never heard? . . . So faith comes from what is heard, and what is heard comes by the preaching of Christ." (Rom. 10:14 and 17) Or, as Luther says it in his commentary on this passage, "Faith is an acoustical affair." Peter verified the method when he claimed that it was "by my mouth the Gentiles should hear the word of the Gospel and believe." The force of this auditory form of interpretation is clear in the story of the Emmaus road appearance of our Lord. Jesus was unrecognized by Cleopas and his companion notwithstanding their possession of all the facts about the history of the Nazarene. Faith in the risen Lord came only after Jesus "interpreted to them in all the scriptures the things concerning himself." (Luke 24:27) And Jesus once-for-all exposed Thomas' type of visual criterion as second-rate when he said, "Blessed are those who have not seen and yet believe." (John 20:29)

What, then, does one proclaim when one communicates the gospel? The New Testament does not leave us in doubt about that. Everywhere the apostles were saying substantially the same thing. They were uttering short, terse, summary statements about the significance of the appearance of Jesus of Nazareth as the Christ. "The God of our fathers raised Jesus whom you killed by hanging him on a tree. God exalted him at his right hand as

Leader and Saviour, to give repentance to Israel and forgiveness of sins. And we are witnesses to these things, and so is the Holy Spirit whom God has given to those who obey him." (Acts 5:30-32) The rather extensive history of the short life of Jesus was summarized in just such pithy proclamations, called in the Greek language, *kerygma*.

Today, the meaning of the Christian faith extends itself into vast and voluminous accounts which occupy great lengths of shelf space. Yet it is known that the rudiments of communication are present in these early reductions. The task of the theologian is to sift through the voluminous account for the authentic kerygma. The task of the witness is to proclaim the kerygma. Such an emphasis on the summation of the gospel in short sentences could, of course, convey a false impression. While the witness of the church took the form of propositions, with acoustical concomitants, essentially the communication was not the spoken word, but the event of speaking the word. The revelation of God came originally in the event of Jesus of Nazareth preaching himself as the presence of God. Judged by any ordinary standard, Jesus was not different from anyone else. But Jesus himself provided the standard by which to judge who he was, for example, Luke 4:18 and 21. Jesus came preaching himself as the preacher, as the revealer, as the truth. Jesus came as the event in which God turns decisively to his people. His words are a part of that larger but more significant event which is Jesus as the Word of God. Everything recorded in the gospels is a reflection of this basic gospel, as dewdrops on grass record the simplicity of the rising Sun. (Martin Kähler) It is possible to read the gospel and to become enamored of the details of Jesus' amazing life. But that could be to miss the synoptic event which is his very significance as revealer of God.

When the friends and followers of Francis Xavier sorted through his letters with the intention of collecting them in a single memorial volume, they hit upon a device reminiscent of the apostolic preaching. They cut the letters in pieces and arranged them in the form of a cross. In this same way, embracing the events and sayings of the life and ministry of Jesus there is the single event of his witness to the truth that in him God was turning decisively to man. The Bible catches this event in short phrases which, when sounded through God's acoustical apparatus in the church, renew the event. "Jesus is Lord!" "Christ died for our sins." "The word became flesh and dwelt among us full of grace and truth." "God was in Christ reconciling the world unto himself."

Now God has entrusted to us the message of reconciliation. "So we are ambassadors for Christ, God making his appeal through us." (II Cor. 5:19, 20) The event of God's revelation in Christ which is the gospel, continues to take place among us when the people of God witness to that event. The witness is itself an event in which God turns again to his people, drawing them into the new age of his presence. The emphasis in the witness is not upon the voluminous account, but upon the fidelity to the vocation as witness.

When Jesus preached himself as the revelation of the Father, the saving event took place in which men knew who God is and to whom therefore they belong. The emphasis here is not upon extensive intellectual content requiring studied consideration, nor upon ideas. Ideas can be pigeonholed. The emphasis is upon a sudden breaking through of divine illumination into the human scene. To that one can only react with the decision of obedience or disobedience. A man's destiny hangs upon his decision.

There is more communication of the gospel in the event of the witness to the lordship of Christ than in theories about Christ's nature. There is more communication of the gospel in the act of preaching than in the content of the sermon. The gospel is communicated more efficiently in the fact of the church's existence than in statements about the nature of the church. And there is more gospel in the phenomenon of a Bible than in the defense of its authority.

Someone recently gave my son a compass. I see it almost anywhere around the house amid the rest of our domestic clutter. Nothing in our house seems to stay in the same place, not even that compass. But the compass always seems to know where it is. Every time I see it, it is pointing in the same direction. This is the impressive thing about the Christian witness. In a world of miscellaneous directions it is the event which, wherever it occurs, signifies the polar event in the destiny of man. No man is irremediably lost as long as there is a Christian witness. And now that there is, men who seek God through other media "are like mariners who voyaged before the invention of the compass." (John Donne)

III. LANGUAGE AND MEANING

What is being suggested here is that there is more communication of the gospel in the steady, faithful witness of the worshipping community—in its reading of the Scriptures, its conduct of the sacraments, its wise and patient instruction and counsel, and its unending chain of prayer—than there is in the effort to establish beachheads for the Christian message on the soil of alien faiths and philosophies. There is more justification for such a position than has yet met the eye. For the Christian gospel is not simply good news which must be proclaimed to be heard. It is *new* news. The gospel is a *new testament*, related to the old not as something more recent, but as something *different*. If it were simply more recent chronologically, there would scarcely be any point at this late date in considering it as something new. However, the gospel still remains new, in the sense of shockingly different. The gospel should still be expected to meet with the reaction it evoked in its earliest form: the sense of scandal, paradox, enmity, and mystery. These are the signs of birth trauma in the movement from the old age to the new.

The main objection pagans had to early Christianity was its newness. Now, usually in order for communication to occur, one must, as Plato said, "presuppose similar mental states." Hence, no one would present *Lady Chatterley's Lover* to a Cub Scout or the works of Paddy Chayevski to a Christopher Fry addict. But when the Christians presented the gospel, it was as if they were talking in a foreign tongue. For this reason many rejected and continue to reject the faith. Karl Jaspers, the German existential philosopher, says such breakdown in communication is a characteristic of the insane, or, as Korzybski the semanticist would say more charitably, it is a sign of the sickness in our language. And indeed, the preaching of the cross was to some foolishness, to others an offense, while being to Christians the power of God unto salvation.

What causes this breach in our communications and how can it be overcome? The most cogent answers to this question lie in the nature of the message itself. One who does not stand within the event of God's turning to man has no positive basis for appreciating the event. Christian communication labors under that handicap for two reasons.

In the first place, the event of the gospel did not emerge genetically out of the past as other events do. Jesus as the Christ was not the historical effect of a series of prior causes. In that sense the gospel event is not ordinary history. By looking at Jesus and hearing his fantastic claims, one cannot conclude to the truth of his claims. Peter confessed that Jesus was "the Christ, the Son of the living God." But "flesh and blood" had not revealed that unto him. Literal, world history does not yield up the mysteries of God's turning to man. Sensitive historians, like artists, can help man clarify his position in the world and help him formulate the questions about his ultimate destiny. As such they are always "the Outsider." They see only enough about history to sound alarm to perils from which history cannot deliver itself. At last, spiritual things are "spiritually discerned." (I Cor. 2:14)

In the second place, the event of the gospel does not come to man as a truth which offers to amend our other truths. It comes as the truth which judges all our partial truths as lies. If men ever had the truth about God, they have it no longer, for "they did not honor him as God or give thanks to him, but they became futile in their thinking and their senseless minds were darkened. Claiming to be wise, they became fools. . . . They exchanged the truth about God for a lie and worshiped and served the creature rather than the Creator." (Romans 1:21-25) In the Biblical story of man, history is not a spiral staircase, but a whirlpool brought on by man's fanatical effort to belong only to himself. Life in history is not a trampolin upon which every step sets us springing higher. It is a bog through which every step is verifying our mortality. As the artist Renoir said late in his life while contemplating a bouquet of flowers: "I have just now discovered the secret of beauty! Is it not a pity that every step of progress in life is a step nearer the grave?"

Christian truth in this setting is indeed a new testament. It comes into history with a suddenness that evokes sheer consternation. "We never saw anything like this!" they said. (Mark 2:12) And it becomes clear to them that they have "seen strange (*paradoxes*) things." (Luke 5:26) There are no old wine skins that can contain this new wine. (Luke 5:37)

How, then, does one overcome the chasm of novelty and unexpectedness in communicating the gospel? He turns necessity into a virtue. He does not attempt to cross bridges where there are no bridges nor set down bridgeheads where the ground is loose. It may be a scandal and an offense to propose Jesus of Nazareth as the one in human history through whom God is turning to man. But that scandal is a wholesome alternative to seductive lies which say "there is only one man in the world and his name is All Men," (Carl Sandburg) or its classical prototype, "Man is the measure of all things." (Protagoras)

> Did we in our own strength confide,
> Our striving would be losing;
> Were not the right Man on our side,
> The Man of God's own choosing.

This very perspective from "the outsider" saves us from the assumption that everything is as we see it. There are some things about which we will remain totally unaware until some outsider calls them to our attention. Estelle in Sartre's play *No Exit* complains that when she cannot see herself she begins to wonder if she really exists. Well, the play is taking place in hell, and there are no mirrors in hell, for hell is any place where there are no possibilities for self-understanding. "I pat myself just to make sure, but it doesn't help much," she confesses. The answer to this predicament is suggested by Sartre in other places: "Without a looker-on a man evaporates!" "The other is the indispensable mediator between me and myself."

Tennessee Williams has a provocative dramatic device which appears with conspicuous frequency in his scripts. One character picks up and inspects an object that has always been within sight of the other character but never really noticed. Immediately thereafter the other character goes to the object and inspects it as if for the first time. The gospel communicates itself to us with this same quality of otherness. It does for us what nothing in our own control could do. It sets our lives within perspectives completely engrossing, yet utterly unanticipated. Kierkegaard has said, no man needs to be told when he has lost a leg, or a wife, or a fortune. But few men seem to notice the loss of a self! The gospel becomes, as the Epistles of James suggests, the mirror in which we see the matters that pertain to our very lostness—or salvation. In that sense it makes contact not with something we already know but with something we do not know at all.

Actually, the problem of communication is somewhat exaggerated if one is limited to the framework which Plato proposed. If the presupposition for communion between two persons is "similar mental states," as Plato claims, then who can ever really communicate anything new! How would one ever ascend from the dimension of existential history to the ultimately hopeful dimension of eschatological history? One must in some way either presuppose a mental state congenial to the gospel he is communicating, or he must provide the condition for the creation of a hospitable mental state. Plato assumed the former possibility in his doctrine of innate ideas. You can recognize almost any good idea because it is already in some sense in your thinking. In that case, there is no such thing as a new idea.

Aristotle took the other way out. Drama and poetry can elicit new mental states. You need no congenial mental state as a presupposition for the communication of a creative artist, for he can sweep you off your feet by the irony and pathos of his work, as humorists evoke your laughter even against your will, although with your concurrence.[1] And inasmuch as thought itself depends for its very existence on language (and not vice versa, as common sense believes), communication does not presuppose similar mental states so much as it presupposes a language evocative of reliable mental states. It seems right to say that if you think the right thoughts you will communicate the right language. Aristotle put it the other way around. In order to think the right thoughts, you must be tutored in the right language.

This structure is helpful to a certain degree in understanding how something so utterly new as the Christian gospel can be meaningful to minds that have not been able to anticipate it. The preaching of the gospel is the "grammar of ascent" by which one is delivered from the whirlpool of history into the elevation of the new age in Christ. The gospel itself provides for the possibility of its own appropriation. Therefore, one does not testify to others with the expectation that their prior acquaintance with the subject will help them understand. One rather testifies with the expectation that what he is saying is providing the conditions for the very understanding of the truth.

And what if others still do not understand? Here the temptations

[1] Stanley Romaine Hopper's book, *The Crisis of Faith*, Abingdon, 1944, was a pioneer in the discussion of Christian communication in historical categories.

are perilous. In desperation or, what is worse, embarrassment, one panics and steps outside the language of his faith for the explanation of his faith. In the act, he loses the very hope others have of understanding him. What does one do if he has just played his original composition and no one understands it? Does he give a lecture on modern music? If he were communicatively efficient, he would simply play it again—not in despair, but joyfully, for he would know that the hope for its understanding is in the playing of it, not in abstract explanations. What does the artist Brancuse do when his bronze masterpiece, "Bird in Space," valued at $35,000, is classed by American customs officers with hospital supplies and kitchen utensils, hence dutiable at forty per cent of value? There may very well be a way of legislating on behalf of art to keep the standards of valuation up to date. Art should not be required to reduplicate the details of evident reality; hence Brancuse's Bird should qualify as art even without head, feet, and feathers. But the communication of the Christian gospel continually waits upon the breaking in of illumination where darkness formerly prevailed. And every time it happens, it is a miracle of the moment.

IV. TRUTH AND DECISION

The Gospel, which is the good news proclaimed by Christians as something new every day, is at the same time the once-for-all news. (Rom. 6:10, Heb. 7:27) It is the final edition. One who hears it should have the same sensations once felt when hearing the voice of a newsboy cracking the night with the latest headline on the war, the elections, or the fights.

If the once-for-all character of the Christian gospel were tied to the sheer fact of a happening in the past, it would be a bit difficult for the Christian communication to sound up-to-the-minute. The truth is, as Luther said, that the gospel is not historical in the sense of a picture which hangs on the wall. It is more like what is known in Marcel Proust's *Remembrance of Things Past* as the "metaphoric memory." It does for time what time does for space: transcends it. Time is telescoped in such a way as to make the event of God's turning to us in Christ a reality of the present moment. The gospel, then, is once-for-all, not in the sense of being located in the irrevocable and irrecoverable past, not in the sense that it can never be repeated. It is final in the sense that it is so full and complete that it can never be rivalled or superseded.

It is fortunate for the Christian witness that this is so. For the event of the witness depends to a great extent on the use of words, and words suffer by the passage of time. Take, for instance, Hegel's illustration. At this moment I jot down the sentence, "Now it is night!" How does this sentence sound when read tomorrow morning? The meaning of the sentence has suffered by the passage of time. But then how do the once-for-all passages in the New Testament sound when put to the same test? "Now is the accepted time!" "I am the way, the truth, and the life." To say that the gospel is the final news is to say that time never stales this event. It is historical in a very unusual sense: not that it is done for, once for all, in the past; it is the repeatable event *par excellence*.

But if the gospel is final in this sense, its language is cast less in the matrix of chronological history and more in the dynamics of present address. The event of God's turning to man in Christ, when expressed propositionally, would sound less like "Washington crossed the Delaware" and more like "I love you." The gospel is the final news in the sense in which a wedding ceremony is final: you date it, as you date Washington's crossing the Delaware; but you commit your future, as in the marriage covenant, and you keep the commitment up-to-date by the repetition of the covenant in daily whispers of self-surrender.

Nor is the gospel final in the sense of being the last truth, as if one thereafter need not seek further for truth. It is not all the news there is; it is simply the best news, the saving truth. For it is the beginning of all truth. It is the perspective that redeems all other truth for us. It is the source and orientation of the meaning of the other truths we hold. Hence, a Christian is not one who deliberately blinds his eyes to the existence of other truths because he has the once-for-all truth. The finality of the Christian truth is rather to him as a lens by which all other truth comes into meaningful focus and coherence. The Christian student does not abandon the university library because he has the truth. The truth in Christ becomes a reading-glass which brings the deceptively fragmentary perspectives of a university library into a single focus.

The net result of witnessing to the final news will be the evoking of decision. The preaching of the gospel requires decision. (Rom. 10:16) Not that the preacher says, "You must decide!" Such language precipitates decisions about whether to decide, losing the very context which makes decision possible. Preaching which properly interprets the gospel is a language which need not *call* for decision because decision is already implicit in its meanings. When final news is heard, filibuster is ruled out and the time for decision is at hand. In the presence of the sudden illumination of the gospel one cannot respond as a character in a Chekhov play, longing wistfully but never acting. "No one who puts his hand to the plow and looks back is fit for the kingdom of God." (Luke 9:62)

This characteristic of the gospel has a real bearing on the desired response to the gospel. If the witness goes about insisting "This is so," he is virtually inviting the response "Prove it!" But the Christian gospel is neither an assertion of facts nor a simple claim to truth, a possible response to which might be skepticism. The Christian gospel is a mobilization of decision. It begins not with a series of facts, but with a call for an act of will. It says, "Do this (and thou shalt live)!" How would stock replies to Christian witness sound in the face of the call to decision? How would "Prove it!" sound in response to, "Do this!" or, "I don't believe it!" in response to "Love thy neighbor!"? One may respond with rejection. He may say, "I will not do it!" But at least the position is then quite clear. A decision has been made in which the hearer has taken a step in determining his destiny. At least he has not been encouraged to filibuster with destiny beyond the deadline for resolution. The Christian gospel divides the world into rebels and disciples. People who parade as skeptics either have not heard the gospel or they have disguised their rebellion in intellectual terms.

V. TRADITION AND TRANSLATION

Finally, the gospel to which Christians witness is official news. It is not invented out of the top of the head and it does not spring from the current situation. It is as venerable as the apostolic witness. The history of the living church is the history of the will to maintain continuity with the apostolic witness. When one is called to witness to the gospel, he is called into a community of interpretation which presupposes an entire history of Christian witness. At the source of this history is the apostolic tradition, the official news, whose mark and authority resides in the way in which it recognizes that the good news is the event of God's turning to history in Jesus of Nazareth.

The meaning of this for Christian communication is not always fully appreciated. It is simply that Christians, for whom witness is an essential part of their lives, are called upon to witness not to their particular experience of the gospel, and least of all to their private opinions about what constitutes the truth. They are called upon in announcing Jesus as Lord to mingle their voices with the prophets and apostles.

That is not to say that some translation is not involved. The responsibility for translation in the act of preaching carries a special urgency, the same kind of urgency playwrights face who know their scripts are not designed to be read, as novels, but to be heard. A man who holds a book in his hands can ponder, leaf back and forth, hold his finger in the place as he consults dictionaries and encyclopaedias. A man who hears a sermon will understand only what he grasps in the moment of its utterance. That is why the preacher must translate. Nothing can be allowed to disrupt the intelligibility of the word he speaks—no archaism, no irrelevancy, no obscurity.[1]

For this same reason, one reads the Bible aloud in public at great peril to communication if he does so without preaching.[2] People who hear the plays of Aeschylus without a knowledge of Greek or the plays of Shakespeare without a knowledge of sixteenth-century life do so at the risk of boredom. Likewise, simply to repeat the phrases of the apostles could be the best way to falsify their witness. Language which is true in one context can be false in another. I recently overheard my son reading aloud from his third-grade exercise book. He came upon the sentence, "Today it is Thursday," stopped, paused, looked up at me and exclaimed, "But it's not!" He was right: it was Tuesday. But he was wrong not to have translated the intention of the author as he read the exercise. Similarly, the Bible without preaching, that is, translation, is not history. It does not yet form the life of the hearer with meaning.

My son did much better at translation on another occasion when I asked him at bedtime if he had brushed his teeth and he replied, "Yes." I subsequently discovered his toothbrush was dry. I ought not have concluded that he lied. Actually, he translated. What he meant to say was, "Dad, I'm too tired to get up and do it now! Let me just go to sleep!" But that proposition would have evoked the wrong response, hence falsified his meaning. Is it not possible to say of the propositions of Christian communication what Aristotle says of prayers? They are neither true nor false. They have rather the intention of moving hearers from one

[1] Cf. Edwin Lewis, *The Biblical Faith and Christian Freedom*, Westminster, 1953.

[2] As the Japanese theologian, Kazoh Kitamori, has said, "The Bible makes no effort to entice the reader." Then he begins his exegesis of the Gospel of Matthew with a beautifully sensitive translation of the evangelical significance of the genealogies, the virgin birth account, and the Herodian purge of male infants. These, he says, usually block an entrance to the Bible as barbed-wire entanglements at one's gate would discourage entrance to one's home. *Logic of Salvation (Kyujyo no Ronri)*, Tokyo, 1953, pp. 128 ff.

dimension of history to another, in the case of the Christian witness, from meaninglessness to meaning, from an inauthentic life
to the covenant with God in Christ, from existential to eschatological history.

When one recommends that the gospel be treated as something
official, he need not be embracing traditionalism. In assuming responsibility to the Christian tradition, one ought to be able to
escape the criticism made by Kathleen Nott of T. S. Eliot, who
allegedly "retrieves the tribal ornaments from the cupboard where
the guest has hidden them, and puts them back on the mantel-
piece." Indeed, there is a dimension of meaning in the Christian
concept of tradition that makes the qualifying adjective "dead"
quite inappropriate. The gospel came not simply in word but in
power. (I Thess. 1:5) It is received not as the word of men, but
as the word of God. (I Thess. 2:13) Everywhere in the New Testament the word of the gospel is associated with something living.

It is true that Jesus did not have a very high estimate of tradition. He called it "the work of men," and discouraged it. (Mark
7:8) But the tradition to which Jesus was referring was a tradition
from which the vitality of prophetism had been squeezed. The
living God had a difficult time communicating his presence through
the pedantry of the Rabbinical religion which Jesus knew. When
the followers of Jesus sensed his resurrection from the dead and
realized he was the word of God incarnate, they knew their words
about him were animated by the vitality of his own triumphant
spirit. Hence, the apostle Paul could say of tradition, it is that
which is "received from the Lord." (I Cor. 11:23; I Thess. 2:13)
The early apostles experienced the vitality of tradition at Pente-
cost. It was when they recollected the holy event of the life of
Jesus that the spirit descended. And when they witnessed to hostile
hearers beyond the circle of the apostolic fellowship, their prayer
of invocation became a highly compressed doctrine of Christian
communication: "And now, Lord, . . . grant to thy servants to
speak thy word with all boldness, while thou stretchest out thy

hand." (Acts 4:29-30) The preacher is not one who opens his mouth to let the Lord fill it. The preacher fills his mouth with the exegesis of the Word that God has given in Christ, in the promise that God will fill the ears of the hearer.

The Protestant Reformers subsequently expressed this truth in a doctrine of the equilibrium of the Spirit and the letter. When the right words are spoken by the Christian witness, God's Spirit animates these words and makes them presently meaningful to the hearer. Thereafter, as Pascal once said, there are only two mistakes that can be made in communication. One is to take everything literally; the other, to take everything spiritually.

The responsibility of Christian witness, therefore, is not designed for one who always wants to get into the act. For the principal actor in Christian communication is not the witness who enunciates the word of truth, but the Spirit of the resurrected Christ who animates the word with life and meaning. If this were not the case, the little story which Kierkegaard tells would have the last word. There was once a circus which caught fire. The director of the circus sent his clown to tell the crowd about the fire. The people, hearing the report from the lips of a clown, believed he was just telling one of his jokes. So they simply sat there, a bit burned up over their inability to tell a prophet from a clown.

Part of the mystery of the gospel is that God always seems to choose some clown to bear witness to it. God, however, unlike the director of the circus, does not leave us clowns to go it alone. He has pledged to make himself heard through the standardized poverty of our vocabularies. When Jeremiah resisted God's call to be a witness, God caused an almond tree to spring up before him. The witness, like the tree, is rooted in vital forces that exceed his own inherent capacity. When Ezekiel was on the verge of saying "No" to God's invitation to a life of witness, God caused him to see wheels within wheels. A technological impossibility! But with God nothing is impossible. It seems paradoxical that God makes his Word known through human words. But that paradox is a paradigm of the power of the Spirit.

CONCLUSION

"When we say Christianity is an historical religion, we do not mean Christianity has a rich experience which emanates from a long historical tradition. We mean it creates history."

YOSHITAKA KUMANO, *Eschatology and Philosophy of History (Shumatsuron to Rekishi Tetsugaku)* Tokyo, 6th edition, 1949, p. 246.

CHAPTER

10

THE MISSION OF THE CHURCH

THE conviction expressed in this volume has been that meaning-ful life, hence the very possibility of history is constituted by the advent of God in Jesus of Nazareth. When the story of God's presence there is told, all moments of time are drawn up into a coherence that transcends them and imparts to them their signifi-cance. Where this eventful meaning is conferred, a community is formed, a community that lives through its enjoyment and through its extension to others of the redemptive meaning.

Contemporary western culture is the frequently ungrateful child of the Hebrew-Christian tradition, however. The significance which its own times have enjoyed is a borrowed significance. For the West has learned from the Biblical tradition that there is an ultimately meaningful life. It has, however, repeatedly abstracted the credit from this tradition without reference to its capital and then gone off to organize life around centers of meaning which rival the Christian coin. The West, and the cultures strongly in-fluenced by the West, has extrapolated structures of meaning from the meaningful event of God's presence and has applied the structures to the future without reference to the event of God's presence, which is the Christian meaning. For that reason it strikes our Western mentality as odd and arrogant when it hears the

235

claim of Christianity that apart from the activity of God history is not possible.

Existential nihilism, therefore, looms as a powerful ally of the Christian movement today. The Christian relevance of existential history is that it reminds mankind that the historical character of human existence is not self-evident. From the perspective of this present age, life could be meaningless, hence despair is a possibility. The current though despairing revolt against all artificial meanings is a cultural event of great importance to the church because it documents in a secular way the Christian conviction that meaning is not humanly apparent. "History only exists in the final analysis for God"[1] because only God can comprehend the totality of events. If God were dead, history would be impossible.

To faith, however, history is divinely constituted. There is a ground of meaning and hence a source of history. When the story of God's presence in Christ is recited, the possibility of history is assured. All the successive events that comprise our life are hinged into a continuous history by "the fulness of time" whose meaning is their coinherence. Without this fulfilled event, our lives are simply process. With it they are purpose. Without it we live toward an ambiguous and uncertain future. With it we know at least that God is in our future and our future is in God. This hope makes history of process.

Eschatological history begins with this revelation, so that everything before this moment is pre-history. "From this moment onwards" (Matt. 26:64, Luke 22:69) our past becomes pre-history, our future is filled with purpose, and our present already has within it the nutriment of the maturest hope. (Eph. 1:14) This is not true because we move through a chronology of events which God is believed to have created and one day will consummate. To say that is to allow the Christian way to yield to the derived and fabricated devices of its cultural stepchild, philosophy of history. Rather, we have history because we live in the presence of the "I

[1] Albert Camus, *The Rebel*, p. 256.

am" in whom past, present, and future are one. (Rev. 1:8; Rev. 22:13) "We have been born anew to a living hope through the resurrection of Jesus Christ from the dead." (1 Peter 1:3) Our pre-history, which was "the times of our ignorance," the time when it was not known that Christ was the fulness of time, God now overlooks. (Acts 17:30-31) All things are now united in Christ. "In him all things hold together." (Col. 1:17) He is the beginning and the end of all things, and he is "at hand." (1 Peter 4:7. Cf. Mk. 1, Gal. 4, Eph. 1) The Christian history is a history which itself creates history. Here indeed is a history that repeats itself. That is the historiographical significance of preaching: Where the word is, there is history.

With the birth of meaning, moreover, community of meaning is created. It is very likely true, though it would be difficult to test, that there is no history where there is but a single individual. In any case, the story of God's saving deed constitutes the church as an eschatological community. The community lives by its recollection simply because when the story is told the fulness of time is at hand. When the story is recited, faith is evoked, for faith is, as Luther said, "an acoustical affair"—it comes by hearing and hearing by the word of God. When the story is enacted through the drama of baptism, one is incorporated into the living body of Christ. When it is enacted through the drama of the Lord's Supper, the many are incorporated into each other and nourished by the real presence of the fulness of the Godhead bodily. Christ is the one loaf upon which the church feeds and in feeding feels its oneness. But in the Lord's Supper the church breaks the loaf as Christ's body was broken for the world. The church will continue to do so "until the Lord come," in order to fulfill the mission which Christ began and for which he gathered the church, to feed the lost sheep. Only after this mission has been fulfilled will the church realize the fulness of what it already appropriates in the Lord's supper. For while in feeding on the loaf the church

feels its oneness, in breaking the loaf the church feels its frag-
mentariness. The body of Christ which was broken for the world
will not satisfy the hunger of the church until the world is with
it at the Lord's table.

I. THE POSSIBILITY OF HISTORY

The creative power of the Christian story, therefore, cannot be
a device for consolidating an orderly society behind what the early
fathers called "the wall of the church." To define the church
without reference to its history-creating mission would be to re-
lapse into the pattern of the old Israel which resisted the Holy
Spirit, making a Temple of what was meant to be a tent, making
a permanent home of what was designed to be a mobile unit.
When the church saw that the Christ was the very hinge of history,
it knew it was called to be a witness and that its history was
destined to be mission. When the glory of God appeared to our
Father Abraham, God said, "Go out." When God appeared to
Moses, he commanded him to "lead forth" the people of God.
When Paul saw the vision of God's universal Lordship in Christ,
he reconstructed the recent past of Israel as a history of default
in mission. (Rom. 9:11) When Stephen saw in Christ the vision
of Heaven as God's throne and earth as his footstool, he branded
the late history of Israel as a history of hard-hearted refusal to "go
out." (Acts 7) Together with the apostles, Paul and Stephen re-
leased impulses which have made the early history of the church
the history of missions. (e.g. The Acts of the Apostles) At the
moment in which our Lord made it clear that all power was given
to him in heaven and in earth, (Matt. 28:18) his followers had
the necessary ingredients for realizing that their response was
synonymous with the commission to "go," making disciples of all
nations. (v. 19) He who has reconciled us to himself has given
us the ministry of reconciliation. "So we are ambassadors of Christ,
God making his appeal through us." (II Cor. 5:20) The church
as mission is the carrier of history. For "how are they to believe

in him of whom they have never heard? And how are they to hear without a preacher? And how can men preach unless they are sent?" (Rom. 10:14, 15) Quite clearly, the church does not remain the church when it salutes its brethren only.

These, then, are the major motifs in eschatological history which together constitute the church's mission: In the presence of Christ the end can be at the beginning. Therefore the Christian witness creates history. But it does so not without constituting a meaningful and responsible community. It becomes the mission of this community to bring God's end, which is Christ, to all peoples in such a way as to constitute their beginning.

Christians live in two times. There is the time of chronos in which one falls forward ambiguously, with no support but his past, which is powerless to be reborn. That is the time of world history. And there is the time of kairos which redeems chronos with the saving support of eternal time, the time God has for us, the time of covenant, sabbath, and salvation—the fulfilled time. That is the time of eschatological history. The point at which the fulness of time is at hand is always our end.

Christian history does not correspond to Charles Peguy's characterization of history as "the elderly general, plastered with medals, brisk and impotent, who reviews the long line of troops laden with their heavy field-kit, on the barrack-square of some garrison town."[1] Christian history is kairos, the time of mobility in which critical turns can be made with facility. Christian history does, of course, lend itself to non-kairos descriptions simply because the church has a chronological life and even continues to live in the old age. But the Christian history is distinctively portrayed only after the image of the minute man. The Christian strikes his tents and burns his boats. The church is the new Israel of God which very easily becomes old again unless it remind itself it is God's perennial child. Kairos, which is the time of the church, easily becomes chronos, old with baldness at its back. But it remains young at

[1] Quoted from his *Clio* in Marcel's *Man Against Mass Society*, p. 28.

the forelock, by which alone it can be grasped.[2] Fixed forms are foreign to its life, its memory is poignant with the mortality of fixed societies (e.g., Rom. 12), and it remains essentially a community without fixed principles. The main flaw which the old cultures found in the Christian movement was its novelty. But the church itself tasted a premature mortality whenever it denied the flaw with the conciliatory distortion that Christianity brings in nothing new (as in Origen, Eusebius, and Tyndall). It is, therefore, quickening to the vitality of the church to remember that whenever the prophets adduced a pattern for the community of God's people they recollected not the kingdom of David and Solomon, but the days in the wilderness. These were the days both of tents and of divine guidance. Forwardness of mind (II Cor. 9:2), which is our readiness to follow God's leading, is likewise the faithful correlate in the life of the Christian people to the fulness of time.

II. THREAT TO EXISTING HISTORIES

What, then, does God require of his people at this moment in world history? In the light of the forces pressing in upon the church, what is the responsibility of the witness? Does God speak to us through the events of our time, revealing the depth of opportunity of the church's task?

When a Christian addresses himself to "the events of our time" he does so in the confidence not that chronos speaks for God, but that kairos transforms chronos into history. The church is commissioned to "go out" because Christ as the fulness of time is the Lord of all events. He is the paradigm which forms the very possibility of an ultimately meaningful history. Speaking to our time is as important to the mission of the church today as speaking to the world was important to God's chosen people in the days of our Lord, and the default as grave. Moreover, there is

[2] A figure from Greek mythology cited by John Marsh in *The Fulness of Time*.

no significant and sensitive speaking to the times which is not preceded by turning to the times.

When the church turns to the times with the question concerning its own responsibility as a church, it hears what it is constituted to hear: "Go ye . . . and preach." In the effort to fulfill that commission under present-day conditions, however, it is running up against a containing wall of ambiguity. The consequences are oppressive for the Christian mission.

One ambiguity is that the church must get very near to the hostile forces of the world in order to be heard by them, yet when it gets too close, it hazards kidnap and silencing. Being "an acoustical affair," however, faith must have a voice.

Another ambiguity is that the church must speak freely, yet it must also accept support from sources alien to its mission. Ironically, the church knows the meaning of this support but those outside the church who judge it do not. The church knows that the state as an order of creation must be left autonomous, free from the control of the church. But the church also knows that the state is an order of redemption at least in the sense that it has more than an obligation for keeping order. It has the responsibility for supporting the conditions that make the free expression of the word of God possible. This truth is often hidden from the state, to the jeopardy of the Christian cause. It is not infrequently forgotten by the church, to the even greater jeopardy of the cause. For the memory of the church records that the dichotomy between church and mission first appeared when the church was granted majority status by the state. It was then that the church whose *esse* was mission became the church *with* a mission. But from that moment to the present the mission has never been free of the suspicion that it is in league with political expansionism.[1] This ambiguity is made the more ambiguous by the realization that "sending" countries are often conspirators in the subjugation of the peoples to whom the mission is being directed. "It is impos-

[1] See Théo Preiss, *La Vie en Christ*, "L'Eglise et la mission," pp. 147 ff.

sible," as Albert Camus has said, "to speak and communicate with a person who has been reduced to servitude."[2]

Still another ambiguity is that wherever the church carries the word, it creates history, but not without re-creating community, and the re-creation of community is a revolutionary threat to all existing communities. This ambiguity shows itself in the collision of two growing forces in the world today, nationalism and the supra-national ecumenical church. When the church tells the nations who they are, it must let them in on the full truth that Christ is their Lord and that because of his Lordship their glory is withering away. The new Israel is destined to supplant the nations. (Rev. 7:9, 21:29, 22:21; Matt. 25:31-33) In this sense the Christian movement is as subversive today as it ever has been in the past. The difference is that governments today have access to more highly developed methods of counter-espionage.

To cite one more ambiguity, the political enforcement of religious pluralism in many quarters of the world is requiring of the Christian movement a curtailment of its propagandistic and proselytizing techniques. This ambiguity may yet turn out in favor of the Christian cause, for the word is most apt to communicate itself when it is allowed to speak for itself. Because of the "missionary rest" in China, for instance, the New Testament is now being read there more and more in the original Greek, rather than in the English with all its emotionally freighted connotations. Yet, when the word is finally heard through these unwittingly lucid means, and when the alien religion is penetrated, there is no way of convincing the protective state that the rules of fair play have not been violated.

In some sense, then, the contemporary situation is forcing upon the church the question of its very survival. This is especially true in countries which are dominated by aggressively atheistic governments and in strongly nationalistic countries where the destiny of the nation is tied to the destiny of a non-protestant faith. I am not

[2] *Ibid.*, p. 250.

at this moment speaking of the problem of the survival of the church as the eschatological community. Socio-political movements are no necessary threat to its existence, for the church is hidden to the world, visible only to faith and to the selective vision of God. I am rather concerned with the empirical body of the people of God which is the bearer of eschatological history in the midst of world history. As the church loses favor with the rising powers all over the world, the efficacy of the body of Christ could become dangerously curtailed. Undeniably, God's cause has been *embodied* —in the church. To treat lightly any abridgment of the church's operations *in extenso* is, therefore, not only bad ecclesiology and bad Christian statesmanship; it is bad historiography. God has linked his mission for history with the witness of the church. Henceforth, faith is an acoustical affair. If it is to be believed, it must have a chance to be heard.

Current anti-clerical movements, however, are revealing to the Christian movement the dialectical character of the church's life. The church both is and is not the body of Christ; it both is and is not the branch of which Christ is the vine; it both is and is not the eschatological community. It can therefore stand pruning not only without loss of its life but with positive gain to its productivity. Kierkegaard's comment in his *Papirer* upon reading Marx's *Communist Manifesto* seems to have become prophetic. The Marxian revolution, he observed, appears to be a socio-economic revolution with a religious aspect. When it comes about, however, it will be found to be a religious revolution with a socio-economic aspect.[3] What is suggested in this commentary is that human history has been going through a phase in which everyone is killing everyone else's gods. This can only ultimately result in religious health for a community whose trust is in the real presence of the God beyond all Gods.

[3] I am indebted to Canon Theologian Howard Johnson of the Cathedral of St. John the Divine in New York for this reference: *Papirer*, X⁶B40, edited by Heiberg, Kuhr, and Torsting; Copenhagen, 1934, citation from 1849.

The pointed question, therefore, in the contemporary situation is not the question of the *survival* of the church so much as the question of its relevancy.

When the church asks itself within the current historical ferment what its responsibility is, it would do well to emulate the early missionary apostles who could summarize the Christian responsibility to the world in one brief charge, "Believe in the Lord Jesus Christ." (Acts 16:31) This is the thing of which the church is most confident, and this is its only incontestable role in the world. But we blunder if we underestimate the breadth of relevance for our world in this simple charge. There are a proliferation of mandates to the church, both negative and positive, in the confession of Christ's Lordship.

Negatively, it means that as a church we must refuse to allow ourselves to be drawn so deeply into the discussions of the time that we lose the very perspective which redeems time, the perspective of the fulness of time. We must refuse to become the mouthpiece or the ideological champion of any social, political, or economic party, program, or interest. The substance of the old age ought not be permitted to continue under the forms of the new age and with its tacit endorsement. We must refuse to undersell the intricacy and complexity of the contemporary problems by proposing simple solutions, such as the patent moralistic, pietistic and humanitarian remedies. A "simple solution" almost by definition would be a solution which by-passes the problem, attempts to solve the problem in terms of the problem, or insist on reforms for which there are inadequate material conditions for their realization.

Positively, the Lordship of Christ means that we must be genuinely prophetic and genuinely redemptive in today's life.

By prophetic I mean we must insist that a maximum of justice be achieved within the concrete conditions of this present time. Because Jesus is Lord, the church cannot live with equanimity in the presence of systems which lord it over people. Prophetism is not ecclesio-monist: it does not require that the world become a church in advance of obeying God. Prophetism is not utopian: it does not cry "peace, peace" when peace-moves are only open gambits for the advance of injustice. Prophetism is not monastic: it does not decline to do something just because it cannot do the perfect thing. Prophetism does not identify politico-cultural achievements with the kingdom of God: the kingdom of God will come on *earth*, but the kingdom of God is the actualization of the Lordship of Christ and not the sum of socio-political gains. Prophetism is not activistic: it does not believe that nothing is being done simply because *men* are doing nothing.

By our redemptive role I mean that we must proclaim the reality of God's mercy to a world from which mercy is always a waning reality. In situations that sting with a variety of tyrannies and to persons for whom hope is a nearly discredited expectation it is good to know that Jesus is really Lord of things. We must participate, through the universal body of Christ, in the miseries of humanity everywhere in the world. It is frightening to speculate on how little Americans, for instance, would know about conditions of life in other parts of the world—world travel, commerce, and diplomacy notwithstanding—were it not for missionaries— their empathy with alien peoples, their documentary correspondence home, and their conscience-quickening furloughs. The church is fulfilling its redemptive mission in the world when the body as a whole becomes patterned after God's own self-emptying in Christ. (Phil. 2)

We must provide an atmosphere of calm and sensitivity in which clear vision and resolute will may be achieved. Above all we must not succumb to the temptation of impatience, losing faith in the very forces that constitute what meaning now supports our life. The Christian life is based primarily on the witness to the presence of God and only secondarily on cries of alarm over his absence. Patience is a situation in which man is willing to do nothing. It must not be confused with indifference born largely of comfort and ease. The patience to do nothing is a grace (H. Richard Niebuhr) conferred upon us by the benevolent awareness that God is present to history. One need not therefore infer that just because man is doing nothing, nothing is being done. There are times when simply to wait is to give God time to do something. While the time of the waiting for God has no room for human manipulation of the mystery in history, it does have room for prayer and fasting, and for the steady witness of the believing community.

INDEX OF NAMES

INDEX OF SUBJECTS